Talent Development and the Global Economy

Perspectives From Special Interest Groups

A Volume in
International Higher Education

Series Editors
Fredrick M. Nafukho and Beverly Irby
Texas A&M University

X

International Higher Education

Fredrick M. Nafukho and Beverly Irby, Editors

Talent Development and the Global Economy:
Perspectives From Special Interest Groups (2017)
edited by Fredrick M. Nafukho, Khali Dirani, and Beverly Irby

Conflict Management and Dialogue in Higher Education:
A Global Perspective (2016)
by Nancy T. Watson, Karan L. Watson, and Christine A. Stanley

Governance and Transformations of Universities in Africa:
A Global Perspective (2014)
edited by Fredrick M. Nafukho, Helen M. A. Muyia, and Beverly Irb

Talent Development and the Global Economy

Perspectives From Special Interest Groups

edited by

Fredrick M. Nafukho

Khali Dirani

Beverly Irby
Texas A&M University

INFORMATION AGE PUBLISHING, INC.
Charlotte, NC • www.infoagepub.com

Library of Congress Cataloging-in-Publication Data

CIP record for this book is available from the Library of Congress
http://www.loc.gov

ISBNs: 978-1-68123-997-2 (Paperback)

978-1-68123-998-9 (Hardcover)

978-1-68123-999-6 (ebook)

Printed in the United States of America

CONTENTS

Foreword .... *vii*

Acknowledgments .... *xi*

1. Why Focus on Talent Development?
   Fredrick Muyia Nafukho, Khalil Dirani, and Beverly Irby..................... *1*

2. Global Talent Flow: International Graduate Students' Career
   Decisions After Graduation
   Sehoon Kim and Soo Jeoung Han.. *7*

3. Leveraging Talent Development in the United States:
   The African American Perspective
   Tomika W. Greer *29*

4. Talent Development and Refugee Women in
   the United States
   Minerva D. Tuliao, Katherine M. Najjar, and Richard J. Torraco *41*

5. The Presence and Skill Circulation of Asian Americans
   Hae Na Kim and Yun-Hsiang Hsu... *61*

6. Maximizing Motivation: Talent Development in
   Nongovernmental Organizations
   Jill Zarestky and Shannon Deer.. *75*

7. Talent Development of Global Virtual Team Leaders:
Challenges and Strategies
Soo Jeoung Han, Shinhee Jeong, and Michael Beyerlein 93

8. Talent Development and the Persistence of Working
Poor Families
Richard Torraco 127

9. Talent Development in the 21st Century and Social Media
Fatemeh Rezaei and Misha Chakraborty 145

10. Talent Development Via Cognitive Mediation
Heidi Flavian 155

About the Authors 171

FOREWORD

I am honored to be asked to write the foreword for this book, *Talent Development and the Global Economy: Perspectives from Special Interest Groups*. The book represents an important contribution to ideas for and about talent development in this age of globalization and the digital and gig economy.

As the former director of research for two training organizations, Zenger-Miller and AchieveGlobal, Inc., as a researcher focused on human resource development, as a current faculty member working with doctoral and masters students in adult and higher education, and as current discipline liaison involved in faculty development, I welcome such new knowledge. Indeed, I wish that such information had been available in the past so that its insights could have been used in my research and put into practice earlier.

The three book editors, Fredrick Muyia Nafukho, Khalil Dirani, and Beverly Irby provide important scholarship and credibility to the text. Fred's work in educational policy analysis within international and comparative education, human capital development, and leadership development make him the ideal person to lead this effort. Certainly, he contributes both scholarly and practical experience to the text. Similarly, Khalil Dirani brings special insights regarding international human resource development and leadership development, with a focus on the Middle East. Although I am not personally acquainted with Beverly Irby, I am familiar with some of her work particularly that in online learning, instructional

Talent Development and the Global Economy:
Perspectives from Special Interest Groups, pp. vii–ix
Copyright © 2017 by Information Age Publishing

leadership, and international leadership. The backgrounds and research of these three co-authors make them the perfect collaborators for this book.

The time and effort involved in writing and editing such a text requires passion for the topic, and it is clear that these three experts have such a passion. All three are involved in different aspects of leadership talent development within international setting. Furthermore, all three are involved in or have conducted research on online learning and development. It is through their combined research and practice that the three recognized the need for such a text. And, we are the beneficiaries.

Not only do the three coeditors bring a wealth of experience, we are privileged to have insights from the various contributors. Certainly, Sehoon Kim and Soo Jeoung Han on international graduate students, Tomika Greer on African Americans, Hae Na Kim and Hsu Yun-Hsiang on Pacific-Islanders, can reflect on their own personal experiences as well as their research work. Minerva Tuliao, Kathy Najjar, Rich Torraco, Jill Zarestky, Shannon Deer. Soo Jeoung Han, Shinhee Jeong, and Michael Beyerlein contribute their knowledge and experience to the various chapters on talent development for specific groupings and organizations. Finally, Fatemeh Rezaei, Misha Chakraborty, and Heidi Flavian present us with important insights regarding the use of new technologies in talent development.

The chapters appear to be organized into four major topical areas. The coauthors begin by providing an argument for the focus on talent development and the global economy. The next section highlights some specific types of individuals within that global picture, namely international graduate students, African-Americans, refugee women, and Asian-Pacific Islanders. Previous literature has not really focused on such individuals; and having these insights will benefit researchers and practitioners. The next section focuses on groups and organizations, such as non-governmental organizations, team leaders in for-profit organizations, and working poor families. These various groups and organizations represent areas of growing interest. The final section emphasizes some new approaches to talent development, specifically social media and cognitive mediation. Again, these provide readers with insights needed for future work.

The ideal audiences for this text include human resource development researchers and practitioners. Both groups can gain important insights to further their work. Another audience would be those researchers and professionals focused on internationalization and globalization and its impacts. They would recognize some important new types of individuals, groups, and organizations for their research and interventions. A third audience consists of those interested in the use of new technology for talent and leadership development. In all of these cases, the audiences would include graduate students, university faculty and administrators, researchers, and practitioners.

Ultimately this book should lead to increased research and improved practice in talent and leadership development. These increases and improvements should influence work not only in the United States but throughout the world. After all, as the coauthors argue, "This is a global economy."

Darlene F. Russ-Eft, PhD
Professor & Discipline Liaison
Oregon State University
Corvallis, Oregon USA.

ACKNOWLEDGMENTS

The editors acknowledge the strong contributions on the authors who bring forth current and critical issues related to global issues and talent development. We also acknowledge the strength that the entities called special interest groups display as they, from the collective body of action researchers, scholar-practitioners, activists, and practitioners move toward an enhanced and functioning workplace. The authors within this body of work call for the basic concept of talent development—that of bold and forward thinking that can be turned to conscious action through learning and talent development.

Talent Development and the Global Economy:
Perspectives from Special Interest Groups, pp. xi–xi
Copyright © 2017 by Information Age Publishing
All rights of reproduction in any form reserved.

CHAPTER 1

WHY FOCUS ON TALENT DEVELOPMENT?

Fredrick Muyia Nafukho, Khalil Dirani, and Beverly Irby

As the world of work changes globally, the number of people working in the on-demand economy, also known as the *gig economy,* is on the rise. Thus the gig economy is characterized by the online marketplace or applications that connect providers or freelancers with customers (Intuit, 2015). According to Intuit, several examples of online services exist that provide products and services to consumers via the Internet including, transportation (Uber, Lyft, GRUB Hub); finding work using online talent marketplaces (Upwork, OnForce, Work Market HourlyNerd, Fiverr); renting out space (Airbnb, Couch Surfing); and miscellaneous services (Task Rabbit, Gig Walk, Wonolo). In this knowledge and gig economy, the demand for talent development is becoming one of the greatest opportunities for profit and benefit, as well as for nonprofit organizations. All over the world, competition for talent poses a number of opportunities and challenges as educationists, trainers, and human resource development experts try to address this critical component for competitiveness and service delivery. Developing a workforce for the 21st century requires strategic talent development policies at institutional, regional, national, and international levels.

Talent Development and the Global Economy:
Perspectives from Special Interest Groups, pp. 1–5
Copyright © 2017 by Information Age Publishing
All rights of reproduction in any form reserved.

Talent has been identified as the only differentiator for an organization, nation, or region's success in this uncertain, complex, competitive, and global environment. Ulrich (2008) defined talent as the equation of 3Cs: Talent = Competence x Commitment x Contribution. Malaeb and Chanaron (2010, p. 2), noted. "*Competence* means that employees have the skills and abilities *today* and *in the future* for required business results ... *Commitment* means that employees are involved and engaged ... while *Contribution* means that employees find personal abundance at occupation." While Ulrich (2008) observed that commitment is focused on meaning and identity and other restraints that tap an employee's heart. In addition, Ulrich and Smallwood (2012) clearly articulated the value of talent on organizations.

This book is unique in many ways, which makes it extraordinary. First, unlike other books that have examined issues of change facing the global economy, no book has examined the issue of talent development from the perspective of special interest groups including the African American perspective; the Asian Pacific Islanders perspective; social media users' perspectives; the perspectives of international students, women refugees, refugees, and nongovernmental organizations; and from the perspectives of for profit, for benefit, and nonprofit organizations. Thus, talent development the world over has become one of the most important issues when it comes to developing human resources, especially through education and training.

This book is divided into 10 thematic chapters including the introductory chapter. In Chapter 2, Sehoon Kim and Soo Jeoung Han examine the issue of talent development from the perspective of international students in higher education. Thus, international graduate students are regarded as prospective talent who can be great assets in increasing the knowledge base within any nation's economy. They emphasize the importance of understanding international graduate students' career decisions after graduation for organizations and countries that are developing a talent pool. Sehoon Kim and Soo examine factors influencing international graduate students' intentions to remain abroad. Through data collected from 499 international graduate students in the United States, a hierarchical multiple regression analysis was conducted. Findings of the study revealed that professor support, home country family ties, and labor market perceptions may be important factors affecting international graduate students' mobility intentions. The study also established that Indian students were more likely to return to their home country than Chinese or Korean students.

In Chapter 3, titled "Leveraging Talent Development in the United States: The African American Perspective," Tomika Greer observes that as an outcome of their involvement in slavery, African Americans have historically had a unique relationship with work compared to other ethnic groups in the United States. Following a variety of concerted efforts to equalize the playing field for African Americans in the workplace, there is still a shortage of African Americans in the highest ranks of leadership in many organizations. Greer considers talent development as a strategy for correcting the existing imbalance in leadership positions. It is argued in the chapter that talent development can only be effective for improving the prevalence of African Americans in leadership positions if organizational leaders are willing to redefine "talent," help African Americans gain access to talent development programs, and include African Americans in the organizational strategy for talent development.

In Chapter 4, Minerva Tuliao, Kathy Najjar, and Rich Torraco explore the talent development of refugee women. They point out that as half of any refugee population, refugee women with varied skills have the potential to contribute to the socioeconomic development of their industrialized countries of resettlement, but face many challenges toward that goal. The chapter addresses the education and training challenges faced by refugee women at the pre-employment stage and how they can be overcome through talent development.

Hae Na Kim and Hsu Yun-Hsiang in Chapter 5 address the issues of Asian Americans' talent development from the career development perspective. They observe that while the number of Asian Americans is growing, there are only a few Asian Americans in leadership positions, and there are certain types of jobs that Asian Americans prefer. The chapter also examines the factors influencing the career choice and development of Asian Americans, and discusses how Asian Americans can diversify their career choices in order to optimally utilize their talents.

Jill Zarestky and Shannon Deer in Chapter 6, "Maximizing Motivation: Talent Development in Non-Governmental Organizations," discuss human resource development practices in general, and point out that talent development in particular is an underresearched topic within nongovernmental organizations (NGOs). They also note that NGOs differ from for-profit and other nonprofit organizations in their missions, structure and operations, management and HRD practices, and employee motivation types and levels. The chapter explores NGO talent development strategies with an emphasis on the specific circumstances and challenges faced by NGOs, and with a view toward sustaining NGO operations across the spectrum of philanthropic, nonprofit, and developmental efforts. In addition, the chapter presents key motivational theories and research on employee motivation in nonprofit versus for-profit companies, and advocates for NGO talent development practices that maximize the opportunities presented by the NGOs' philanthropic missions and their highly motivated employees.

In Chapter 7, titled "Talent Development of Global Virtual Team Leaders: Challenges and Strategies," Soo Jeoung Han, Shinhee Jeong, and

Michael Beyerlein focus on globalization of the economy and development of communications technology, which has led to growth in the use of work teams with members in multiple countries resulting in increased multiculturalism in the distributed virtual workplace. The chapter identifies factors that affect the processes and performance of nationally/culturally diverse teams in a virtual environment and discusses the strategies that leaders can use to develop their global virtual teams. The authors identify a set of challenges for global virtual team leaders and suggest tangible strategies for overcoming the identified challenges.

Chapter 8 by Rich Torraco, titled "Training Development and Working Poor Families in the United States," addresses the persistence of working poor families and the causes and consequences of this problem. According to Torracco, a working poor family is one in which at least one adult family member works full time for a full year, but despite the wages earned, mostly from low-wage work, the family remains in poverty and is unable to attain basic financial security. The chapter examines the issue of the working poor in the United States and discusses relevant aspects of this problem; in the United Kingdom comparisons are also drawn with other developed nations to show the severity and prevalence of the problem. It is pointed out that the persistence of working poor families has three major causes: educational barriers faced by the working poor, recent changes in the job and labor market, and rising economic inequality.

In Chapter 9, titled "Talent Development via Cognitive Mediation," Fatemeh Rezaei and Misha Chakraborty discuss the role of social media in developing talented employees within an organization. They provide pertinent information showing why it is important to consider social media as a potential source for talent development in today's workplace. In addition, the chapter examines practices that are offered by researchers and practitioners regarding the role of social media in talent development. Also addressed in the chapter are the potential benefits and positive outcomes from the use of social media in the training and development systems of organizations.

Chapter 10 is written by Heidi Flavian who points out that when referring to one's talent, people usually refer to one's specific ability to cope with a variety of challenges in a specific domain. Moreover, they assume that this specific talent is an individual quality one is born with. Flavian correctly argues that in recent decades, researchers and theoreticians have developed a variety of approaches for developing people's talents while focusing on cognitive mediation. Their main claim is that although people are born with talents in a variety of domains, it is up to educators and the environment to provide students with the proper cognitive tools to realize all their talents and use them as effectively and efficiently as possible. The chapter demonstrates that cognitive mediation for talent development is essential for all learners.

REFERENCES

Intuit. (2015). *Intuit forecast: 7.6 million people in on-demand economy by 2020.* Retrieved from http://investors.intuit.com/press-releases/press-release-details/2015/Intuit-Forecast-76-Million-People-in-On-Demand-Economy-by-2020/default.aspx

Malaeb, R. C., & Chanaron, J. J. (2010). *Talent management DNA.* Retrieved from http://www.ufhrd.co.uk/wordpress/wp-content/uploads/2010/08/1_21.pdf

Ulrich, D. (2008). Call for talent: What is the best solutions? *Leadership Excellence, 25*(5), 17.

Ulrich, D., & Smallwood, N. (2012). What is talent? *Leader to Leader, 63,* 55–61.

CHAPTER 2

GLOBAL TALENT FLOW

International Graduate Students' Career Decisions After Graduation

Sehoon Kim and Soo Jeoung Han

Globalization has influenced individuals, organizations, and societies both positively and negatively (Marquardt, 2007). One of the prominent phenomena resulting from globalization is the global mobility of highly skilled or educated people, so-called talent. Academic discourse on talent mobility and its impact has existed for several decades mainly with two contrary views. First, it is regarded that talent mobility leads to negative consequences for individuals through underemployment or unemployment (Fan & Stark, 2007; Moorhouse & Cunningham, 2010) and for home countries by a lack of human capital in organizations and society (Lianos, 2007). Another viewpoint focuses on the positive impact of talent mobility, such as individual career development (Donnelly, 2009), the good use of a migrant's remittance (Le & Bodman, 2011), and contributions to both home and host countries through knowledge sharing (Beine, Docquier, & Rapoport, 2008).

Due to the unique economic, social, and individual contexts of talent mobility, it is difficult to simply conclude what causes individual mobility

Talent Development and the Global Economy:
Perspectives from Special Interest Groups, pp. 7–27
Copyright © 2017 by Information Age Publishing
All rights of reproduction in any form reserved.

or how the negative impacts can be minimized. However, there is a general consensus that maintaining a talent pool and developing those who have potential are critical to winning the global competition (Athey, 2008; Collings & Mellahi, 2009). From a national perspective, graduate students are regarded as prospective talent who can be great assets in increasing the knowledge base within a nation's economy (Grubel & Scott, 1966; Vinokur, 2006). Through studying abroad, graduate students can be talent for either host or home countries. First, the mobility of graduate students can provide an opportunity for many countries to develop their future talent (OECD, 2014). For instance, small or less-developed countries whose educational system is not well-equipped may rely on advanced foreign institutions to educate their country's future leaders. On the other hand, for host countries international student enrollment not only increases the profit of higher education, but also plays a strategic role in expanding and developing a national talent pool. Developing and retaining highly educated international students are increasingly important for developed countries to sustain their leadership edge in academic and industrial research and development (Johnson, 2002; Vinokur, 2006).

In the United States, international students are 29% of the total graduate program enrollment and the majority of those students study engineering, science, business, or education (OECD, 2014). Approximately 25% of international students enrolled in higher education stay in the host country for work-related reasons after graduation (OECD, 2011). Researchers have found that highly educated migrants have been involved in producing scientific studies and patents that significantly contributed to economic and social development in the United States (Hart, 2006; Wadhwa, 2009). To some extent, therefore, the supplies of talent in a country are likely to depend on whether or not international graduate students return to their home country after receiving a quality education abroad (Freeman, 2010).

Given that the higher the educational level of student migrants, and the stronger the impact on the society and organizations in the home and host countries (Saravia & Miranda, 2004), it is important to understand how international graduate students decide to remain in a foreign country or return to their home country after graduation. As the world is more globalized, and competition for talent among countries has intensified, scholars have drawn considerable attention to the mobility of international graduate students (Dumont, Spielvogel, & Widmaier, 2010). Many researchers have focused their studies on highly educated students' mobility were conducted from the perspective of economics (e.g., Dreher & Poutvaa, 2011; Güngör & Tansel, 2008; Musumba, Jin, & Mjelde, 2009). However, there are few researchers who have investigated what influenced international students' intentions to remain abroad or return home, focusing on individual psychological perceptions (Baruch, Budhwar, & Khatri, 2007;

Szelényi, 2006). Baruch et al. (2007) created an extensive conceptual model of factors influencing intentions to remain abroad and tested it with international students in the United Kingdom and the United States, but the sample included only undergraduate students in business. Szelényi (2006) used a qualitative approach by interviewing 26 international graduate students and had difficulty excluding the influences of individual contexts from the results because the participants had various nationalities, majors, and demographics.

We designed our study to examine what affects international graduate students' intentions to remain in the United States after graduation. Specifically, we identified factors that influenced international students' career decisions from the literature and tested the relationships between those factors and students' intentions. As the main concerns of talent development include effectiveness and structural systems for development (Garavan, Carbery, & Rock, 2012), how the process for international students ended up may provide guidance for research and practices in human resources (HR) and talent development. We expect that the results of our study will be useful for HR professionals to better understand prospective talent and to establish a broad talent development strategy. First, the significance of this study, from an individual perspective, lies in international graduate students' career development, because whether staying or leaving the decision may considerably influence individual careers. Second, at organizational and national levels, mobility issues of the highly educated are related to managing and developing global human resources. Given the competition for talent and dependence on foreign human resources in many countries, developing and retaining international graduate students can be a top priority for many organizations and countries.

THEORETICAL FRAMEWORK

To perform a deliberate behavior in the future, people generally make a plan. This careful and proactive decision process is defined as intention (Bandura, 2001; Fishbein & Ajzen, 1975). Self-motivation that occurs during the intention process is the key source of effort to perform a behavior (Fishbein & Ajzen, 1975). When individuals have stronger intentions to engage in a behavior, the possibility of actions for the behavior tends to be higher (Ajzen, 1991).

According to the theory of planned behavior (Ajzen, 1991, 2011), an intention as the most decisive factor of a behavior is created based on three types of considerations: behavioral, normative, and control beliefs. First, behavioral beliefs refer to the possible outcomes of the behavior and the assessment of the outcomes. Next, normative beliefs are the normative expectations of others and motivation for these expectations. Last, control beliefs are regarding factors that may help or hinder performing the behavior. These beliefs are affected mainly by individual characteristics or circumstantial settings, such as personality, social contexts, culture, and other sources of information (Ajzen, 2011). In a similar vein, the social cognition theory (Bandura, 1986; Bratman, 1999) also contends that individuals formulate their thinking based on the influences of others within the social context, and intentions can be attuned, revised, or completely changed when new information or experiences are received during social activities.

Given these theories related to the intention process, we assume that international students' intentions to remain abroad may depend on social experiences with people in the host or home countries and environmental conditions. First, when international students believe that their life in the host county is satisfactory, their intentions to remain abroad may become stronger. This behavioral belief of the theory of planned behavior may be affected by students' impressions of a university and relationships with people around them. For example, international students' impressions of the level of support from professors and fellow students can generate a positive belief toward the host country and its people. The study found that assistance and care from professors and fellow students influences international students' decisions about their careers (Van Dick et al., 2004). For this reason, many universities in the United States offer supportive programs for new international students to enhance their academic and campus-life satisfaction (Arthur & Flynn, 2011). Therefore, we argue that the level of support from people in the host country such as professors or students will influence international graduate students' choice of staying in the host country in the near future. Based on such an understanding, we hypothesized that:

Hypothesis 1a: The support from professors will be positively associated with international graduate students' intentions to remain in the United States

Hypothesis 1b: The support from fellow students will be positively associated with international graduate students' intentions to remain in the United States.

A strong relationship with parents or siblings in the home country may lead to social pressure for them to return to the home country in the future. As this normative belief of the theory of planned behavior may negatively influence international students' intentions to remain, we regarded family ties with the home country family as a critical factor that may influence the decision to remain in the host country. Several researchers have found that strong family ties reinforced tendencies to return to home countries (Black, Gregersen, Mendenhall, & Stroh, 1999; Dowling & Welch, 2004). Baruch et al. (2007) discovered that family relationships weakened the inclination of international college students to remain in the host country. In the light of these studies, we formulated a hypothesis as:

Hypothesis 2: The relationship between international graduate students and their home country families will be negatively associated with students' intentions to remain in the United States.

Regarding control beliefs of the theory of planned behavior, since a future job is an important matter for international graduate students, how they perceive job opportunities in the host or home countries may influence whether they intend to remain abroad or return to the home country. Several studies found that perception of job opportunities in the host country was a key motivator for international students to remain in their host country (e.g. Baruch et al., 2007; Szelényi, 2006). Tansel and Güngör (2003) found that the possibility of employment in the host country was the most important reason for delaying the return home for Turkish students who were studying abroad. This phenomenon is similar to how foreign workers are attracted by the economic market of the host country (Carr, Inkson, & Thorn, 2005). As people from developing countries desire to work in developed countries in order to obtain better incomes and higher standards of living (Carr et al., 2005; Creehan, 2001; Djalal, 2001; Sani, 2000), we supposed that many international students may expect to obtain a job in the United States after graduation, if an opportunity arises. On the other hand, job opportunities in the home country may affect international students' return intentions. As many host country governments and organizations consider international graduate students as their future talent, aggressive recruitment may be implemented because of competitive work conditions. Given that students' expectations for the labor market in either host country or home country play influential roles in their futures (Arthur & Flynn, 2011), we hypothesized that:

Hypothesis 3a: Perceptions of the U.S. labor market will be positively associated with international graduate students' intentions to remain in the United States.

Hypothesis 3b: Perceptions of the home labor market will be negatively associated with international graduate students' intentions to remain in the United States.

The nationality of the international students may also be an important factor influencing the intentions to remain in the host country after graduation (Cantwell, 2011). China, India, and South Korea are known not only as fast growing economies, but also as the top three countries that send students to the United States (OECD, 2014). The rapidly improving economic conditions in the home countries may increase the number of students who desire to go back to their home countries after graduation because of the increased job opportunities and income levels (World Bank, 2015). In this regard, Baruch et al. (2007) found mixed results depending on the countries. The majority of students from East Asia (e.g. China and Korea) were likely to return to their home country soon after completing their studies, while the majority of Indian students desired to remain in the host country for at least a few years. Decisions about remaining in or leaving the host country may be influenced by gaps in the quality of life between the host and the home countries because the expectations of better standards of living is a major factor affecting migration (Campbell, 2007; Semela, 2011; Tansel & Güngör, 2003). The GDP per capita using purchasing power parity calculations for Korea and China was about $29,000 and $10,000, while that of India was about $4,800 in 2011 (World Bank, 2015). Hence, we suggest the following hypothesis:

> **Hypothesis 4:** International graduate students' intentions to remain in the United States will differ by nationality (China, India, or South Korea). Students from China and South Korea will have lower intentions to remain in the United States than students from India.

METHODS

The primary goal of this study was to examine factors that influence international graduate students' intentions to remain in the United States after completing their education. To this end, we conducted a questionnaire survey that involved variables for predicting students' intentions. A self-administered design was employed as it is appropriate in measuring perceptions of individuals.

Sample and Data Collection

The population of interest for this study included all international graduate students ($N = 3,499$) who attended a state university located in the southern United States during the fall 2011 semester. We randomly selected

1,677 out of 3,355 international graduate students and sent an email with a link to the electronic survey. As the response rates of online surveys are typically less than traditional survey approaches, we employed techniques for increasing participation, such as prenotice emails and multiple reminders. In total, 499 students responded to the survey for a response rate of 30% and 446 respondents fully answered the questionnaire.

Respondents were from 54 countries (see Table 2.1), primarily representing China (26.4%), India (22.0%), Korea (13.8%), Iran (4.0%), Mexico (3.2%), and Taiwan (3.0%). The majority of student studied engineering (52.1%), agriculture and life sciences (11.4%), and science (9.4%). Among the respondents, 60.1% answered that they were in the doctoral program and 70.3% were not married. Regarding length of stay, 26.5% had been in the United States for less than one year and 21.2% had been in the United States for more than four years.

Table 2.1. Nationality of the Respondents

Nationality	*Frequency*	*Percentage*
China	133	26.5
India	114	22.2
Korea	69	13.8
Iran	20	4.0
Mexico	16	3.2
Taiwan	15	3.0
Other countries	126	25.2

Note: Other countries with more than five students included Brazil, Colombia, Egypt, Indonesia, Japan, Nigeria, Peru, Thailand, and Turkey.

Measures

As this study followed Baruch et al.'s (2007) conceptual model of the decision to stay abroad, some of the measures used in their previous study were adopted. In the case of using Baruch et al.'s instruments, we revised words to better fit our study's context, such as removing the terms United Kingdom and changing the university name. In addition, we changed the Likert scale levels to four-point scales to provide consistency between questions and to measure more thoughtful and decisive data without midpoint ratings. Several demographic questions were also included in a separate section.

Labor Market Perception

Labor market perceptions in the home country and United States, such as employment prospective and career development, were posed using five statements developed by Baruch et al. (2007). Respondents were asked to indicate the extent of agreement with each statement on a four-point scale ranging from (1) strongly disagree to (4) strongly agree. A sample item was: "I have a good chance of getting a good job in the United States." The Cronbach's alpha for the measure on the home country and the United States was 0.67 and 0.68, respectively.

Family Ties

To measure the relationship with home country family, the scale developed by Baruch et al. (2007) was used. There were four statements about the relationship with the respondents' family and the importance of family in their life. Respondents were asked to indicate their level of agreement with each statement. A sample statement was, "I miss my family when I stay in the United States." The Cronbach's alpha for this scale was 0.73.

Professor Support

In this study, we adopted the professor support scale developed by Pearce, Sommer, Morris, and Frideger (1992). The scale had five statements that pertained to support from or relationships with professors. A sample item was, "I can rely on my professors." The Cronbach's alpha for this scale was 0.77 in this study.

Student Support

This five-statement scale was developed by Pearce et al. (1992) and consisted of support from or relationships with fellow students. A sample item was, "My fellow students seem willing to listen to my problems." The Cronbach's alpha reliability score for this scale was 0.72.

Intention of Staying Abroad

As our dependent variable, we measured intentions of international students to remain in the United States with the question, "How long would

I like to stay in the United States after graduation?" The participants' answers were chosen from four options: "not at all," "for a short while," "for some while," and "as long as possible." Although the use of multi-item scales is generally considered typical practice in social science, a carefully created single-item measure can be as valid as a multi-item one (Bergkvist & Rossiter, 2009). When the purpose is to measure an overall psychology, a single-item scale can be a good measurement (Fuchs & Diamantopoulos, 2009). In this research, we also valued the practical advantages of using a single-item scale, such as parsimony, ease of administration, and a higher response rate (Fuchs & Diamantopoulos, 2009).

Demographic Variables

We involved five demographic items to be controlled in the question-naire based on the related literature: length of stay in the United States, current major, current degree, marital status, and children. As the number of respondents who answered married but the spouse is not in the United States was small (4.7%, $n = 21$), the marital status variable had two levels (single and married) without further dividing.

DATA ANALYSIS

Cronbach's alpha values for labor market perception were lower than the commonly accepted range of greater than .70 (Nunnally, 1978). However, an alpha between .50 and .70 can be acceptable (Caplan, Naidu, & Tripathi, 1984; Tuckman, 1999) and low coefficients may not mean that there is a problem with the construction (Spiliotopoulou, 2009). As those alphas are close to .70 and it is up to the researchers' determination of how much error we were willing to tolerate given the specific purpose and circumstance (Pedhazur & Schmelkin, 1991), we included those scales in our statistical analysis, given that those measures were recently developed and because of this study's exploratory characteristics. For data cleaning, we identified that the pattern of the missing data is probably missing completely at random (MCAR), using Little's MCAR test ($p > .05$). Although the ratio of the missing data was about 11% (53 out of 499), we chose the listwise deletion method because it has an advantage in using a multivariate technique and MCAR (Meyers, Gamst, & Guarino, 2013).

We analyzed descriptive statistics focusing on the overall tendencies of students' intentions. A correlation coefficient analysis was conducted to find bivariate relationships between variables. A hierarchical multiple regression was applied to estimate the prediction of factors for the intentions to remain abroad. The dependent variable was students' intentions of remaining in the United States. The first step of the independent variables included five control variables and the second step included five main variables measured by multi-item scales. In the multicolinearity diagnosis, the variance inflation factors (VIF) among all the variables were below 2.00 and the tolerances were above .60, indicating that the predicting variables were not highly correlated. In addition, an ANOVA was used to examine the differences among the three countries that send the most international students to the United States (China, India, and Korea) regarding students' intentions to remain in the United States. In case of significance in the analysis, Tukey's HSD is a statistical approach that is widely used for an ANOVA post-hoc test. The term as it is will be understood for readers who learned statistics.

RESULTS

Overall, 9.7% of the students answered that they would like to return to their home country right after graduation, 23.5% wanted to remain for a short while, 46.8% wanted to remain for some while, and 20.0% indicated they would like to remain in the United States as long as possible. Table 2.2 provides means, standard deviations, and correlations among the study variables. The table revealed several noteworthy relationships among the predictor variables. It was interesting that students' majors, their perception of other students' support, and perception of the U.S. labor market reported by the international graduate students were unrelated to their intentions to remain in the United States. However, students' intentions to remain in the United States was significantly related to their length of stay in the United States, degree, marital status, children, relationship with family, support of professors, and home labor market perceptions. Among the hypothesized predictor variables, students' perceptions of their home labor market had the strongest correlation with students' intentions to remain in the United States.

A two-step hierarchical regression was employed to explore the predictors of graduate students' intentions to remain in the United States. The results, presented in Table 2.3, indicated that support from professors was a strongly positive predictor of intention to remain in the United States ($\beta = .21, p < .05$), supporting Hypothesis 1a. However, support from fellow graduate students was not associated with intention to remain in the United States ($\beta = .08$, ns), therefore, Hypothesis 1b was not supported.

We found that the family tie was negatively correlated with the intention to remain in the United States ($\beta = -.20, p < .05$). As shown in Table 2.3, the relationship between international students and their home families

Table 2.2. Descriptive Statistics and Correlations Between Variables

Variable	M	SD	1	2	3	4	5	6	7	8	9	10
1. Length of stay	2.83	0.87	–									
2. Degree	1.61	0.49	0.38**	–								
3. Major	4.69	1.94	0.00	-0.16*	–							
4. Marriage	1.30	0.46	0.25**	0.23**	0.08*	–						
5. Children	3.41	2.37	0.07	-0.03	-0.04	-0.02	–					
6. Family ties	3.34	0.53	0.01	-0.01	0.06	0.22**	-0.01	–				
7. Professor support	3.04	0.48	0.01	0.04	0.05	0.14**	0.01	0.17**	–			
8. Students support	2.97	0.41	-0.07	-0.04	0.01	0.04	0.03	0.14**	0.51**	–		
9. U.S. labor market	2.60	0.59	-0.02	-0.07	-0.04	-0.05	0.05	0.05	0.22**	0.27**	–	
10. Home labor market	2.07	0.69	-0.09*	-0.07	0.03	0.05	-0.06	0.29**	0.13**	0.17**	0.00	–
11. Intention to remain	2.78	0.87	0.13**	0.08*	0.02	0.11**	0.09*	-0.13**	0.11*	0.05	0.04	-0.23**

Note: Degree (1 = master's, 2 = doctoral), Major (1 = Engineer, Science, Geo Science, 2 = others), Marriage (1 = married, 2 = single), Children (1 = no child, 2 = have children).

*$p < .05$, **$p < .01$

Table 2.3.   Results of Hierarchical Multiple Regression Analyses Predicting Intentions of Remaining in the United States

	Intention to Remain in the United States[a]	
Variable	Model 1	Model 2
Length of stay	.05 (.03)	.04 (.03)
Degree	.06 (.09)	.03 (.09)
Major	.03 (.09)	.04 (.09)
Marriage (single)	.16 (.09)	.21* (.09)
Children	.24 (.126)	.20 (.12)
Professor support		.21* (.10)
Students support		.08 (.11)
Family ties		−.20* (.08)
U.S. labor market		.02 (.07)
Home labor market		−.27** (.06)
	.03*	.11**
		.08**

Note: a Estimates are standardized regression coefficients (B) with standard errors in parentheses; n = 471.

* $p < .05$, ** $p < .01$

accounted for 4% of significant variance in the intention to remain in the United States, supporting Hypothesis 2. We found that the perception of the U.S. labor market was not significantly correlated with international graduate students' intentions to remain in the United States ($\beta = .02$, ns, see Table 2.3), providing no support for Hypothesis 3a. On the other hand, the results showed that the perception of the labor market of the home country was negatively related to the students' intentions to remain in the host country ($\beta = -.27$, $p < .01$), supporting Hypothesis 3b. Thus, we can conclude that the more positive the labor market perception of the home country, the less likelihood of students' intentions of remaining in the United States.

Of the control variables, marriage was significant, with married couples reporting higher intentions to remain in the United States ($\beta = .21$, $p < .05$). This result showed that single students have a greater possibility of staying a shorter time in the United States than do married students. However, as shown in Table 2.3, other control variables such as length of stay, degree, major, and children were not significant predictors for the dependent variable.

To test whether there is any difference in international graduate students' intentions to remain among Chinese, Indian, and Korean students, we conducted an ANOVA. The study found that foreign students' intentions to remain in the United States were significantly different depending on the country they were from. The ANOVA results showed a significant effect of an individual's nationality on the intention to remain in the United States (F $(2, 308)$ = 4.95, $p < .05$). In addition, we compared where the difference was among those countries. Since the main effect was found to be statistically significant, we performed a post hoc test to determine which pair of means was statistically different using Tukey's HSD. The result indicated that international graduate students from China and Korea were more likely to have higher intentions to remain in the United States after completing their studies compared with students from India. Therefore, Hypothesis 4 was partially supported.

DISCUSSION

As international graduate students are regarded as prospective global talent, how to attract and develop them may be one of the important matters for national and organizational competitiveness. Many countries and companies are confronted with a lack of talent in the near future because of the retiring baby boomer generation, low birthrates, and global competition for highly-skilled workers (Athey, 2008; Tarique & Schuler, 2010). While embracing international students is regarded as one of the solutions for talent deficiency (Freeman, 2010), countries that send young elites abroad for educational and professional development may be deprived of a source for future development if those students do not return to their home countries. Given the value of international graduate students, it is important to investigate how those students intend to remain abroad or return to their home countries after completing their studies.

We conducted a quantitative study using a questionnaire survey approach to examine the factors that influence international graduate students' intentions to remain in the United States after graduation. The sample for this study was 499 international graduate students attending a state university in the United States. As a result, approximately 10% answered they would like to go back to their home country after graduation while 20% wanted to remain in the United States for as long as possible. The results of the bivariate correlation and multiple regression analyses partially espoused our hypotheses which were developed based on three types of intention considerations: behavioral, normative, and control beliefs.

Professor support was related to the students' intentions to remain in the United States. Unlike the study of Baruch et al. (2007), student support was not associated with intention to remain. We deduced that these outcomes were because of graduate students' characteristics of less interaction with fellow students than undergraduate students. For graduate students, while their social activities tend to be more limited than those of undergraduate students on campus, relationships with professors may have more impact on their career decisions and professional development. Another speculation is prevalent university-wide support programs for international students that are more effective than individual, informal, and sporadic support by fellow students (Arthur & Flynn, 2011; Shen & Herr, 2004). These results are related to behavioral beliefs that assistance and care from professors may influence international graduate students' satisfaction and positive expectations regarding living and studying abroad and, in turn, increase their intentions to remain in the United States.

We found that the relationship with the home country family is negatively associated with international students' intentions to remain in the United States. This may be due to international students' normative beliefs in which they should be with or support their home country family in the future (Ajzen, 2011, Dowling & Welch, 2004). Taking into account the significant relationship with marriage, home country family ties may be attributed to a social pressure or responsibility for international students to fulfill their family roles (Reynolds & Constantine, 2007).

International graduate students' intentions to remain were significantly related to the perception of the home country labor market, but were not related to that of the U.S. labor market, partly supporting our hypotheses and the previous research (Baruch et al., 2007; Szelényi, 2006; Tansel & Güngör, 2003). These results are related to control beliefs in the theoretical framework in which job opportunities in the host or home countries may control whether students intend to remain abroad or return to the home country. When international students expect a good opportunity to obtain a job in their home country, they were likely to leave the United States while the prospect of a job in there, negligibly predicted students' future decisions. There are several possible reasons for the nonsignificant relationship between the perception of the U.S. labor market and intention to remain. First, international students' initial career expectations could influence their intentions (Güngör & Tansel, 2008). As they probably recognize that most international students return to their home country after graduation, their initial plans may not include serious consideration of working abroad. Second, it is likely that students' intentions to remain were affected by the U.S. economy. We collected the data during 2011 when the U.S. economy was weakened. Third, international students may acknowledge the difficulty of obtaining a working permit. Regardless of their desire and the general labor market condition, positions that sponsor an H1B visa may be limited (Tung & Lazarova, 2006) and this perhaps led to no significant relationship between the U.S. labor market perception and intentions to remain.

Regarding the comparison among the three main countries that send the majority of students to the United States, Indian students were more likely to return to their home country than Chinese or Korean students, not supporting our hypothesis and Baruch et al.'s (2007) study. This unexpected result puzzled us, but one probable cause was found in the students' demographics. It was found that most Chinese and Korean students were married while most Indian students were single. Marriage was one of the significant predictors for the student's intention in our regression analysis, and previous research also indicated that the social role of marriage is an important factor affecting individual beliefs and attitudes (Biddle, 1986; Lazarova, Westman, & Shaffer, 2010). Therefore, the country comparison result might be greatly influenced by students' marital status in each country. In this study, due to the insufficient number of participants to test marital status's influence by country, further investigations could not be conducted. Future research may involve a more balanced sample of international graduate students and examine how intentions to remain are different if the marital status is controlled.

Practical Implications and Future Trends

The practical implications of this study underscore the role of HRD, which should involve not only individual development, but also economic, political, and social development worldwide (Marquardt, 2007; McLean & McLean, 2001). First, to develop talent and a talent pool, detailed and promising career plans should be discussed and provided for international graduate students at the individual, institutional, and national levels. Because international graduate students' decisions to remain in or leave the host country likely depend on whether or not they are employed, it may be necessary to assist international graduate students in locating resources for them to research appropriate career directions and job opportunities.

For host countries, if highly educated internationals are essential to develop a national workforce, host country governments may need to provide friendly immigration policies and laws so that international graduates can remain longer and be employed without obstacles. Financial support for the home country family and generous vacation policies may be necessary to increase the settlement of highly educated human resources in host country organizations. In addition, academic support to help international students adapt to the school environment and develop their ability can potentially enhance students' satisfaction with their new lives that can positively influence their intentions to remain. As this study found, faculty may play an important role as mentors, coaches, and role models for international graduate students, and they need to know how to help international students deal with their problems. Given the concerns and circumstances of international graduate students, customized and specific aid programs that are different from those for undergraduate students may be necessary.

On the other hand, for home countries, sponsored programs by the home government or domestic organizations, which include a mandatory return clause, may be encouraged. When international students return to their home country, the gains include not only human resource capacities, but also intangible resources of advanced knowledge and skills. Offering quality jobs and providing suitable compensation may increase return rates of highly educated migrants. The governments may need to have a better understanding of the highly educated human resources that reside in their foreign countries. Tracking what is going on with their international graduate students who are in and outside their country may enable the home government to establish a countrywide workforce supply plan in an effort to stabilize their talent pool.

For organizations in home countries, the potential for continuous interest in hiring and developing highly educated students in foreign countries is ongoing. Internships, sponsorships, programs to support both students and their families, and regular contacts from organizations may increase international students' intentions of returning to their home country and employment. Even though some international graduate students do not return to their home country right after graduation, maintaining a relationship with those students is potentially beneficial for the home country because brain drain is transformed into brain gain when they eventually return home with advanced knowledge and experiences.

LIMITATIONS AND RECOMMENDATIONS FOR FUTURE RESEARCH

There are limitations in this study. First, the research model did not sufficiently account for the dependent variable. The effect size of the regression model was as low as that of Baruch et al. (2007). This implies that the variables used in this study may not be enough to predict student mobility plans. In other words, although social support (from professors and fellow students), family ties, and the labor market can be factors affecting intention to remain, there may be something else that plays a crucial role in the decision process. Extensive explorations may be needed to find factors that influence the international graduate students' intentions to remain. We found possible factors from the expatriate research about influences of successful performance in international assignments and repatriation. Some of them include cultural adaptation, satisfaction with the host country, spouse's satisfaction with living in the host country, and children's education plans (Caligiuri & Lazarova, 2002; Konopaske, Robie, & Ivancevich, 2005; Lee, 2007). In addition, the mobility plans of international graduate students who are preparing for and concerned about their future may be greatly affected by coaching, mentoring, and counseling for careers provided by the university, host country, and home country.

Second, we did not include the impact of initial career development plans on individual mobility intentions. For international graduate students, going abroad to study might be a critical decision in their lives. Many of them probably deliberated about their postgraduate careers with a vision. As Güngör and Tansel (2008) found, their initial plans before mobility may considerably account for the international students' intentions after graduation. We suggest that future research should ask international students about their initial plans for whether or not they plan to return and investigate how the host country experience affects their initial plans.

Third, we investigated international graduate students in a single state university in the southern United States. The particular characteristics of the population may have influenced the results, because students' inclinations are likely to be impacted by the policies and culture of the institution, region, and society (Evans, Forney, Guido-Dibrito, Patton, & Renn, 2010). For a more extensive application of the research, future researchers may include additional universities in various cultures, regions, or countries so that they can provide more generalized findings.

Last, two of the psychometric measures used in this study provided relatively low Cronbach's alpha values. To enhance the reliability of these measures, the statements may need to be scrutinized to increase clarity. Adding more statements in each measure can also help improve the consistency of the measures. Future researchers may need to bolster the measures for international students' migration intentions.

CONCLUSION

Studying abroad in graduate programs is regarded as one of the prominent global talent development approaches. As highly educated students are key in prospective human resources for organizations in host and home countries, concerns about how to develop and retain these future talents may be great for many organizations and governments. We found that professor support, home country family ties, and labor market perceptions may be important factors affecting international graduate students' mobility intentions. These factors may have great implications for college programs and a national talent development strategy.

REFERENCES

Ajzen, I. (1991). The theory of planned behavior. *Organizational Behavior and Human Decision Processes, 50*(2), 179–211.

Ajzen, I. (2011). The theory of planned behavior: Reactions and reflections. *Psychology & Health, 26*(9), 1113–1127. doi:10.1080/08870446.2011.613995

Arthur, N., & Flynn, S. (2011). Career development influences of international students who pursue permanent immigration to Canada. *International Journal for Educational and Vocational Guidance, 11*, 221–237. doi: 10.1007/s10775-011-9212-5

Athey, R. (2008). It's 2008: Do you know where your talent is? Connecting people to what matters. *Journal of Business Strategy, 29*(4), 4–14. doi:10.1108/02756660810886953

Bandura, A. (1986). *Social foundations of thought and action.* Englewood Cliffs, NJ: Prentice-Hall.

Bandura, A. (2001). Social cognitive theory: An agentic perspective. *Annual Review of Psychology, 52*(1), 1–26.

Baruch, Y., Budhwar, P. S., & Khatri, N. (2007). Brain drain: Inclination to stay abroad after studies. *Journal of World Business, 42*(1), 99–112. doi:10.1016/j.jwb.2006.11.004

Beine, M., Docquier, F., & Rapoport, H. (2008). Brain drain and human capital formation in developing countries: Winners and losers. *Economic Journal, 118*(528), 631–652. doi:10.1111/j.1468-0297.2008.02135.x

Bergkvist, L., & Rossiter, J. R. (2009). Tailor-made single-item measures of doubly concrete constructs. *International Journal of Advertising, 28*(4), 607–621. doi:10.2501/S0265048709200783

Biddle, B. J. (1986). Recent developments in role theory. *Annual Review of Sociology, 12*, 67–92.

Black, J. S., Gregersen, H. B., Mendenhall, M. E., & Stroh, L. K. (1999). *Globalizing people through international assignments.* Reading, MA: Addison-Wesley.

Bratman M. E. (1999). *Faces of intention: Selected essays on intention and agency.* New York, NY: Cambridge University Press.

Caligiuri, P., &Lazarova, M. (2002). A model for the influence of social interaction and social support on female expatriates' cross-cultural adjustment. *International Journal of Human Resource Management, 13*(5), 761–772. doi:10.1080/09585190210125903

Campbell, E. K. (2007). Brain drain potential in Botswana. *International Migration, 45*(5), 115–145. doi: 10.1111/j.1468-2435.2007.00429.x

Cantwell, B. (2011). Academic in-sourcing: International postdoctoral employment and new modes of academic production. *Journal of Higher Education Policy and Management, 33*(2), 101–114. doi:10.1080/1360080X.2011.550032

Caplan, R. D., Naidu, R. K., & Tripathi, R. C. (1984). Coping and defense: Constellations vs. components. *Journal of Health and Social Behavior, 25*, 303–320.

Carr, S. C., Inkson, K., & Thorn, K. (2005). From global careers to talent flow: Reinterpreting 'brain drain.' *Journal of World Business, 40*(4), 386–398. doi:10.1016/j.jwb.2005.08.006

Collings, G. D., & Mellahi, K. (2009). Strategic talent management: A review and research agenda. *Human Resource Management Review, 19*, 304–313. doi:10.1016/j.hrmr.2009.04.001

Creehan, S. (2001). Brain strain. *Harvard International Review, 23*, 6–7.

Djalal, D. (2001). Business the Bali way. *Asian Business, 37*, 70.

Dowling, P. J., & Welch, D. E. (2004). *International human resource management* (4th ed.). London, England: Thomson.

Dreher, A., & Poutvaara, P. (2011). Foreign students and migration to the United States. *World Development, 39*(8), 1294–1307. doi: 10.1016/j.worlddev.2010.12.001

Dumont, J. C., Spielvogel, G., & Widmaier, S. (2010). *International migrants in developed, emerging and developing countries: An extended profile.* (OECD Social, Employment and Migration Working Papers No.114). Paris: OECD. Retrieved from http://www.oecd.org/els/mig/46535333.pdf

Evans, N., J., Forney, D. S., Guido-Dibrito, F., Patton, L. D., & Renn, K. A. (2010). *Student development in college: Theory, research, and practice.* San Francisco, CA: Jossey-Bass.

Fan, C. S., & Stark, O. (2007). International migration and "educated unemployment." *Journal of Development Economics, 83*(1), 76–87. doi:10.1016/j.jdeveco.2006.05.002

Fishbein, M., & Ajzen, I. (1975), *Belief, attitude, intention, and behavior: An introduction to theory and research.* Reading, MA: Addison-Wesley.

Freeman, R. B. (2010). Globalization of scientific and engineering talent: International mobility of students, workers, and ideas and the world economy. *Economics of Innovation and New Technology,* 19, 393–406. doi:10.1080/10438590903432871

Fuchs, C., & Diamantopoulos, A. (2009). Using single-item measures for construct measurement in management research. *Die Betriebswirtschaft, 69*(2), 195–210.

Garavan, T. N., Carbery, R., & Rock, A. (2012). Mapping talent development: Definition, scope and architecture. *European Journal of Training and Development, 36*(1), 5–24. doi:10.1108/03090591211192601

Grubel, H. B., & Scott, A. D. (1966). The international flow of human capital. *The American Economic Review, 56*(1/2), 268–274.

Güngör, N. D., & Tansel, A. (2008). Brain drain from Turkey: An investigation of students' return intentions. *Applied Economics, 40*(23), 3069–3087. doi:10.1080/00036840600993999

Hart, D. M. (2006). From brain drain to mutual gain. *Issues in Science & Technology, 23*(1), 53–62.

Johnson, J. M. (2002). The reverse brain drain and the global diffusion of knowledge. *Georgetown Journal of International Affairs,* 3, 125–131.

Konopaske, R., Robie, C., & Ivancevich, J. M. (2005). A preliminary model of spouse influence on managerial global assignment willingness. *International Journal of Human Resource Management, 16*(3), 405–426. doi:10.1080/0958519042000339570

Lazarova, M., Westman, M., & Shaffer, M. A. (2010). Elucidating the positive side of the work-family interface on international assignments: A model of expatriate work and family performance. *Academy of Management Review*, *35*(1), 93–117. doi:10.5465/AMR.2010.45577883

Le, T., & Bodman, P. M. (2011). Remittances or technological diffusion: Which drives domestic gains from brain drain? *Applied Economics*, *43*(18), 2277–2285. doi:10.1080/00036840903153838

Lee, H. (2007). Factors that influence expatriate failure: An interview study. *International Journal of Management*, *24*(3), 403–413.

Lianos, T. P. (2007). Brain drain and brain loss: Immigrants to Greece. *Journal of Ethnic & Migration Studies*, *33*(1), 129–140. doi:10.1080/13691830601043562

Marquardt, M. J. (2007). Globalization: Fight it, or embrace and purify it? *Human Resource Development Quarterly*, *18*(3), 285–291. doi:10.1002/hrdq.1205

McLean, G. N., & McLean, L. D. (2001). If we can't define HRD in one country, how can we define it in an international context? *Human Resource Development International*, *4*(3), 313–326. doi:10.1080/13678860110059339

Meyers, L. S., Gamst, G., & Guarino, A. J. (2013). *Applied multivariate research: Design and interpretation*. Thousand Oaks, CA: Sage.

Moorhouse, L., & Cunningham, P. (2010). Permanently 'in process': The intersection of migration, work identity and the reality of human resource development in the South African context. *Human Resource Development International*, *13*(5), 587–597. doi:10.1080/13678868.2010.520483

Musumba, M., Jin, Y. H., & Mjelde, J. W. (2009). Factors influencing career location preferences of international graduate students in the United States. *Education Economics*, *19*(5), 501–517. doi:10.1080/09645290903102902

Nunnally, J. O. (1978). *Psychometric theory*. New York, NY: McGraw-Hill.

OECD. (2011). *Education at a glance 2011*. Retrieved from www.oecd.org/dataoecd/61/2/48631582.pdf

OECD. (2014). *Education at a glance 2014*. Retrieved from http://www.oecd.org/edu/Education-at-a-Glance-2014.pdf

Pearce, J. L., Sommer, S. M., Morris, A., & Fridger, M. (1992), *A configurational approach to interpersonal relations: Profiles of workplace social relations and task interdependence*, Working Paper, Graduate School of Management, University of California, Irvine.

Pedhazur, E. J., & Schmelkin, L. P. (1991). *Measurement, design, and analysis: An integrated approach*. Mahwah, NJ: Erlbaum.

Reynolds, A. L., & Constantine, M. G. (2007). Cultural adjustment difficulties and career development of international college students. *Journal of Career Assessment*, *15*(3), 338–350. doi:10.1177/1069072707301218

Sani, R. (2000). New study by ministry to stem IT brain drain. *New Straits Times-Management Times*, *5*, 15.

Saravia, N., & Miranda, J. (2004). Plumbing the brain drain. *Bulletin of the World Health Organization*, *82*, 608–615.

Semela, T. (2011). Vulnerability to brain-drain among academics in institutions of higher learning in Ethiopia. *Asian Social Science*, *7*(1), 3–18. doi:10.5539/ass.v7n1p3

Shen, Y., & Herr, E. L. (2004). Career placement concerns of international graduate students: A qualitative study. *Journal of Career Development, 31*(1), 15–29. doi:10.1023/B:JOCD.0000036703.83885.5d

Spiliotopoulou, G. (2009). Reliability reconsidered: Cronbach's alpha and pediatric assessment in occupational therapy. *Australian Occupational Therapy Journal 56*, 150–155. doi:10.1111/j.1440-1630.2009.00785.x

Szelényi, K. (2006). Students without borders? Migratory decision-making among international graduate students in the U.S. *Knowledge, Technology & Policy, 19*(3), 64–86. doi:10.1007/s12130-006-1030-6

Tansel, A., & Gungor, N. D. (2003). "Brain drain" from Turkey: Survey evidence of student non-return. *Career Development International, 8*(2), 52–69.

Tarique, I., & Schuler, S. R. (2010). Global talent management: Literature review, integrative framework, and suggestions for further research. *Journal of World Business, 45*(2), 122–133. doi:10.1016/j.jwb.2009.09.019

Tuckman, B. W. (1999). *Conducting educational research*. Fort Worth, TX: Harcourt Brace.

Tung, R. L., & Lazarova, M. (2006). Brain drain versus brain gain: An exploratory study of ex-host country nationals in central and east Europe. *International Journal of Human Resource Management, 17*(11), 1853–1872. doi:10.1080/09585190600999992

Van Dick, R., Christ, O., Stellmacher, J., Wagner, U., Ahlswede, O., Grubba, C., … Tissington, P. A. (2004). Should I stay or should I go? Explaining turnover intentions with organizational identification and job satisfaction. *British Journal of Management, 15*(4), 351–360.

Vinokur, A. (2006). Brain migration revisited. *Globalisation, Societies & Education, 4*(1), 7–24. doi:10.1080/14767720600554957

Wadhwa, V. (2009). A reverse brain drain. *Issues in Science and Technology, 25*, 45–52.

World Bank. (2015). *World Bank open data*. Retrieved from http://data.worldbank.org/

CHAPTER 3

LEVERAGING TALENT DEVELOPMENT IN THE UNITED STATES

The African American Perspective

Tomika W. Greer

INTRODUCTION

"If you don't work, you will steal." —Granddaddy R. J. Wilson (born 1917).

"If you don't work, you don't eat." —Grandmama Madie Hogan Wilson (born 1923).

My paternal grandparents, R. J. and Madie Wilson, were married in 1938 and reared 13 children in segregated Mississippi in the 1930s, 1940s, 1950s, and 1960s. R. J. and Madie worked hard as sharecroppers. While they never amassed a lot of material possessions, they left a legacy of love and hard work to their children and their 45 grandchildren. Anyone who

Talent Development and the Global Economy:
Perspectives from Special Interest Groups, pp. 29–39
Copyright © 2017 by Information Age Publishing
All rights of reproduction in any form reserved.

knows the Wilson family knows that R. J. and Madie built a very tight-knit family who take pride in being Wilsons. They have taught their family to value hard work and to have little tolerance for poor work ethic. R. J. passed away in 1991, and Madie passed away in 2005. Of the many stories that Wilson family members still tell, the favorite memories are of R. J. and Madie assigning household chores to anyone who crossed the threshold of their home, especially their grandchildren. At any given time during a family reunion, there is discussion over R. J.'s belief that if you don't work, you will steal; and Madie's paraphrase of 2 Thessalonians 3:10, which also suggests the necessity of working.

R. J. and Madie Wilson are examples of how beliefs about the role of work have been passed down from one generation to the next generation in the African American community. Though they had very little formal education, R. J. and Madie possessed a skillset that allowed them to successfully grow and harvest crops and provide for their family. Such a skillset is less relevant to many African Americans in the 21st century. As the work that African Americans perform has evolved, so have their needs in terms of how to become good workers and employees. Therefore, I examined talent development from an African American perspective. Specifically, herein, I describe the evolution of work among African Americans and advocate for the importance of their being included and having access to talent development efforts in organizations. Ultimately, I advocate for talent development as a means of improving the prevalence of African Americans in organizational leadership positions.

BACKGROUND

African Americans have historically had a unique relationship with work compared to other ethnic groups in the United States. Africans were first brought to the United Stated in 1619 (Jordan, 1962). They were brought to the United States for the purpose of labor—to work. However, their work was unlike the work assigned to other groups of people. Africans eventually became enslaved to service *for life* and their offspring were to inherit the same type of work obligation (Jordan, 1962). This slavery was based merely on their membership in the African race.

Following the abolishment of slavery in 1865, people of African descent began to slowly gain the rights and freedoms of other people in the United States but were often stigmatized by their work in service-oriented jobs. For instance, in the 1960s, Madie Wilson could be found cleaning the homes of White families in Mississippi. It was not until the 1970s and 1980s when affirmative action efforts related to affirmative action law began to dictate that qualified African Americans move into more professional positions and presumably up the corporate ladders.

But, affirmative action was largely about numbers of minorities in the organizations and complying with federal laws. There was little thought exerted towards supporting the beneficiaries of affirmative action to progress into leadership positions in the organizations. Though affirmative action was initially thought to be a positive move towards helping African Americans to move away from the stigma of their years of forced servitude and into equal opportunities with the hegemonic groups, these efforts did nothing to address the need for talent development among African American employees in professional positions. Instead, the few African Americans who were promoted remained concentrated in the lowest ranks of management (Kalev, Kelly, & Dobbin, 2006). As Thomas (1990, p. 6) noted, "minorities no longer need a boarding pass, they need an upgrade. The problem is not getting them in at the entry level; the problem is making better use of their potential at every level, especially in middle-management and leadership positions. This is no longer simply a question of common decency; it is a question of business survival."

Ultimately, compliance with affirmative action laws increased the numerical representation of African Americans in the United States workforce. However, they failed to alter the organizational policies, practices, and climate that initially kept African Americans out of these organizations. As a result, the organizational climates precluded African Americans from enjoying the same career development opportunities and rewards for their contributions to the organization as their White counterparts enjoyed (Agócs & Burr, 1996).

The inauguration of President Ronald Reagan initiated the decline of affirmative action mandates. By the end of Reagan's presidency in 1989, affirmative action was essentially dead (Leonard, 1990). In place of affirmative action, organizations introduced diversity management in the 1990s (Kelly & Dobbin, 1998). Diversity management was the first effort to correct the imbalance of people of color in the higher ranks of management and leadership in the workforce. Diversity management "is primarily concerned with improving interpersonal and inter-group communication and relationships in the workplace" (Agócs & Burr, 1996, p. 36). The goals of diversity management were accomplished by emphasizing awareness of differences and learning to appreciate differences while letting go of negative stereotypes. However, diversity management—in this sense—did nothing to address the organizational cultural artifacts, structures, systems and beliefs that create and reinforce the lack of African Americans in the higher ranks of leadership in their organizations. Furthermore, diversity management emphasizes the view that all employees are unique individuals, suggesting that everyone is "diverse." This viewpoint waters down the reality that there are power structures in American society and in the work-place that put members of specific groups at a disadvantage in terms of opportunities and recognition (Agócs & Burr, 1996).

In the 21st century, talent management has been introduced as the contemporary means by which organizations will optimize their human capital in hopes of creating strategic advantage over their competitors. Talent management includes the set of policies and practices that define how organizations strategically attract, select, develop, and manage their employees. Talent development is a specific process within talent management that "focuses on the planning, selection and implementation of development strategies for the entire talent pool to ensure that the organization has both the current and future supply of talent to meet strategic objectives and that development activities are aligned with organizational talent management processes" (Garavan, Carbery, & Rock, 2012, p. 6).

Talent development represents the most recent mechanisms by which African Americans could be developed for positions at the top of their organizations. However, talent development efforts exist within the organizational culture that has sustained the structures and beliefs that preclude African Americans from the top leadership positions. As a result, the primary talent development concerns for African Americans become gaining access to talent development opportunities and inclusion in organizational strategies for talent development.

RECOGNIZING AFRICAN AMERICANS AS "TALENT"

There is not a universal consensus as to what constitutes talent in the context of talent development (Nilsson & Ellström, 2012). However, to understand and implement talent development processes, it is important to define talent to determine "who should be developed, to what degree, and in what way" (Garavan, Carbery, & Rock, 2012, p. 14). As a result, talent has been defined by researchers in a large variety of ways. In each case, researchers have defined talent in a way that suits the purposes of their view of the goals of talent development. Indeed, organizations typically design and implement talent development processes that are unique to their organizational needs (Garavan, Carbery, & Rock, 2012). Ultimately, how talent is defined in an organization will dictate the organization's talent development strategies.

One view of talent is an inclusive approach that "suggests that all employees should be regarded as great talent given their potential to generate creative ideas" (Garavan, Carbery, & Rock, 2012, p. 7). This view of talent includes "the potential of all employees, who are to be managed and guided to achieve high performance levels by the human resource function in an organization" (Nilsson & Ellström, 2012, p. 30). By viewing talent in this wider sense, organizations could potentially implement talent development processes to benefit all employees rather than an elite few. This approach is consistent with the idea that organizations should support equitable opportunities for career development so that all employees will achieve their full potential as an employee (Byars-Winston, 2014). However, few organizations view talent in this inclusive sense (Garavan, Carbery, & Rock, 2012). Organizations that view talent from this wider perspective are likely not offering talent development programs that prepare employees for high-level leadership positions. It simply is not feasible to develop every employee to become a company executive.

However, the popular practice of viewing talent as "a limited pool of organizational members who possess unique managerial and leadership competencies" (Garavan, Carbery, & Rock, 2012, p. 7) does not seem to fit with the philosophy that talent can and should be developed. These employees are "sought, recruited, and differentially rewarded without regard to their specific roles in an organization" (Nillson & Ellström, 2012, p. 29). In the case of African American employees, this narrow and exclusive view of talent is particularly problematic because of the historic affirmative action mandates. Employees who are thought to have gained employment through affirmative action initiatives are perceived as less competent and less likely to progress up the organizational ladder than their peers (Heilman, Block, & Lucas, 1992). There remains a stigma in the workplace about groups of people who were historically assisted in employment by affirmative action laws. Members of these groups are viewed as less competent; and therefore, would be less likely to benefit from talent development processes when talent is defined as a small selection of hand-picked employees.

For various reasons, African Americans are less likely to engage in talent development programs when the view of talent is more narrow. First, when the hand-picked "talent" is subjectively identified by organizational leaders, this puts African Americans at a disadvantage because they may not have anyone in leadership positions who will advocate for their inclusion in talent development programs. Organizational leaders are likely to select those individuals who they have mentored or networked with. In many cases, these selected employees will be similar to the organizational leaders in terms of gender and ethnic background. And while such selection may not be intentional, organizational leaders are likely to choose certain employees because they see a little bit of themselves in the junior employee and want to help that person reach their full potential.

Moreover, when talent development is a process designed for the elite few in the organization, there tends to be a quota for the number of employees that can engage in the talent development programs. When African

Americans are not at the forefront of organizational leaders' minds, they may continuously be passed over for talent development opportunities in favor of other employees, usually White men.

GAINING ACCESS FOR AFRICAN AMERICANS TO TALENT DEVELOPMENT OPPORTUNITIES

Gaining access to talent development opportunities is paramount for African American employees, so that they receive the training and development necessary to reach the highest levels of organizational leadership. But, in the American society and many workplaces, systemic discrimination and unconscious bias prohibit African Americans' access to talent development opportunities by supporting traditional employment practices that pre-date African Americans' widespread entry into the professional workforce (Kalev, Kelly, & Dobbin, 2006). "These traditional practices tend to create privilege for those who were (and remain) in a position to establish and regulate workplace policies, practices, and culture, and disadvantage for women, racial minorities, people with disabilities and aboriginal peoples" (Agócs & Burr, 1996, p. 31). For African American employees to gain access to talent development opportunities, deeply rooted organizational structures and beliefs will have to be changed. However, this is a long and deliberate process that requires an intentional focus on upsetting the long-standing status quo.

In changing the organizational culture, priority has to be given to establishing a more inclusive definition of talent and seeking new, innovative ways to identify talent. I advocate for a more inclusive definition of talent, because this will help organizational leaders to think more broadly about where talent may reside in the organization. I am not suggesting that African Americans cannot fit the widely-used definition of talent that includes the perceived high potential employees, but I do believe that in many cases, organizational leaders are more likely to identify with someone like themselves and select those individuals to benefit from talent development programs.

Regarding innovative ways to identify talent, it is not enough for organizational leaders to rely on networks, social encounters, or even performance evaluations. All of these criteria encourage subjective assessments that promote selection of an in-group for talent development opportunities. It is not sufficient to only look to previously-identified, "high potential" employees for inclusion in talent development programs because those selections are often made within a context of unconscious bias that systematically excludes African American employees (Byars-Winston, 2014). Instead, organizations can establish a selection process in which all employees can apply for talent development programs. Organizations should make known to all employees what talent development opportunities exist within the organization. If there is only a certain number of employees that can take advantage of those opportunities, all eligible employees should be invited to submit an application for the program. Ideally, applications would be reviewed and scored by a neutral third-party so that employees can be selected for the program based on their application and fit for the program rather than who they know or don't know within the organization.

INCLUDING AFRICAN AMERICANS IN ORGANIZATIONAL STRATEGIES FOR TALENT DEVELOPMENT

Kalev, Kelly, and Dobbin (2006) argued that to truly make a difference in introducing diversity into organizational leadership, it is important to assign diversity efforts as someone's primary responsibility in the organization. This idea was also supported with empirical evidence as having staff and/or a committee devoted to diversity and inclusion significantly improved the odds of being in management for black women and black men (Kalev, Kelly, & Dobbin, 2006). I offer that a similar approach should be utilized to ensure that African Americans are included in organizational strategies for talent development. There should be an organizational leader who is specifically tasked with considering the talent development needs of African American employees in the organization. This leader should be responsible for setting goals, developing a course of action, and evaluating their progress regarding including African Americans in talent development programs (Kalev, Kelly, & Dobbin, 2006). Furthermore, this leader should be accountable to an executive in the organization to promote alignment between organizational needs and the need to include African Americans in organizational strategies for talent development.

To effectively include African Americans in organizational strategies for talent development, organizations must consider the development needs of African Americans within the specific context of their organization. Such consideration is particularly feasible when a competency-based approach to talent development is used. A competency-based approach allows the organizational leaders to assess the needs of the organization to reveal the competencies required to optimize organizational productivity and/or effectiveness. The organization can also assess the competency gaps in individual employees to determine how best to develop each employee. This approach could be advantageous for African American employees, because it forces the organization to look at them as individuals and recognize their strengths, weaknesses, and value to the organization. Ultimately, organizations will have to examine their biases and assumptions about who or what talent is and how it can be developed in an equitable manner (Byars-Winston, 2014).

FUTURE TRENDS

When African Americans gain access to talent development programs and are included in organizational strategies for talent development, organizations are likely to see an increase in African Americans at higher levels of management in their organization. This occurrence will hopefully create a more established pipeline of African American leaders as the organizational norms and behaviors begin to change. To create this pipeline, talent development programs have to be effective for African American employees. Essentially, organizations will have to development and implement culturally-responsive processes that do not merely seek to convert all employees to the White male standard of leadership and development (Kelly & Dobbin, 1998). All employees will not fit this mold but, they can still be effective leaders. Indeed, if all leaders were to conform to the White male standard, the ethnic diversity of top leadership will never substantially change. Accordingly, even those employees who do not necessarily conform should be granted opportunities to further develop their talent, benefitting themselves and their organizations.

Talent development programs that include and support the advancement of African Americans are likely to include four leadership competencies: knowledge and skill development, confidence and empowerment, ownership and commitment, and sociopolitical acumen (Aponte-Soto, Ling Grant, Carter-Johnson, Colomer, Campbell, & Anderson, 2014). Knowledge and skill development will be the cornerstone of the talent development efforts as African American employees learn the technical skills needed to do their jobs more effectively in alignment with their expertise and organizational goals. Confidence and empowerment should become an essential aspect of talent development efforts for African American employees because of the lack of representation at higher levels of management. African American employees can be empowered by realizing that their diverse status is not a hindrance to their advancement but, instead is celebrated as an asset by their organization. Furthermore, for African Americans to lead in organizations, they will need to have confidence and be empowered to take ownership for the success of the organization which will result in high levels of commitment to the organization. When African Americans begin to take ownership and increase their commitment to the organization, they will be better positioned to change the organizational cultural norms that have historically kept African Americans out of the higher ranks of the organization. Finally, by enhancing their sociopolitical acumen, African

Americans will be better positioned to create and sustain the networks and relationships that will help them to advance within their organizations and professions.

Cultivating talent development opportunities that support confidence and empowerment, ownership and commitment, and sociopolitical acumen in African Americans will help to eradicate the environmental and contextual barriers (Byars-Winston, 2014) to advancement that plague African American employees. These environmental and contextual barriers are the by-product of the many of years of separate and unequal status of African Americans. The barriers are often unconscious but, deeply rooted in our culture. When organizations begin to use talent development processes as a means of eliminating these barriers, we will begin to see the pipeline of African Americans moving through the corporate ranks that was envisioned in the early days of diversity management but, has yet to be realized.

While it is vital for organizational leaders to recognize their biases and work towards more inclusive talent development programs that can benefit African American employees, talent development practices are undergoing a shift from organizational responsibility to individual responsibility (Garavan, Carbery, & Rock, 2012). In the contemporary age of protean and boundary-less careers, the responsibility of talent development is beginning to fall more on the individual employee. As a result, African American employees will need to be proactive in their pursuits of talent development opportunities. This will likely involve some self-assessment exercises that help African American employees to identify their own gaps in skills, knowledge, and competencies; and seek to fill those gaps. It will also require that African American employees ensure that they are abreast of what opportunities exists and how they may benefit from engaging in those opportunities. Ultimately, it will be important for African American employees to advocate for themselves in addition to organizations doing their part to include African Americans in talent development programs.

CONCLUSION

The relevance of work in the African American community has historically been of central importance. From the days of slavery when the value of African Americans was in their ability to work and produce to the mid-20th century when African Americans continued to excel and take pride in their work in agriculture and service. As affirmative action made inroads for African Americans in the latter part of the 20th century, the current U.S. workforce is filled with African Americans in professional jobs with little representation in upper management. The lack of African Americans in these positions can be traced back through historical perceptions that African Americans are less qualified, less capable, and less competent.

It is critical that talent development programs be leveraged to help correct the imbalance of power in these organizations. However, for talent development programs to be effective in correcting this issue, African American employees must gain access to available talent development opportunities and be considered in the organizational strategies for talent development. To achieve these goals, several changes in the organizational structure, processes, and beliefs must occur.

I have outlined some ideas for why talent development is critical for African American employees and how African Americans can gain access to talent development opportunities and be included in organizational strategies for talent development. My hope is that through this work, I will spark dialogue about the current state of talent development as it pertains to African Americans, given their unique history with work in the United States. Ultimately, I would like to see this dialogue result in tangible actions that destroy the status quo and propel African Americans more proportionately up the corporate ladder.

REFERENCES

Agócs, C., & Burr, C. (1996). Employment equity, affirmative action and managing diversity: assessing the differences. *International Journal of Manpower, 17*, 30–45.

Aponte-Soto, L., Ling Grant, D. S., Carter-Johnson, F., Colomer, S. E., Campbell, J. E., & Anderson, K. G. (2014). Championing culturally responsive leadership for evaluation practice. In P. M. Collins & R. Hopson (Eds.), *Building a new generation of culturally responsive evaluators through AEA's Graduate Education Diversity Internship program. New Directions for Evaluation, 143*, 37–47.

Byars-Winston, A. (2014). Toward a framework for multicultural STEM-focused career interventions. *The Career Development Quarterly, 62*(4), 340–357.

Garavan, T. N., Carbery, R., & Rock, A. (2012). Mapping talent development: Definition, scope, and architecture. *European Journal of Training and Development, 36*, 5–24.

Heilman, M. E., Block, C. J., & Lucas, J. A. (1992). Presumed incompetent? Stigmatization and affirmative action efforts. *Journal of Applied Psychology, 77*, 536–544.

Jordan, W. D. (1962). Modern tensions and the origins of American slavery. *The Journal of Southern History, 28*, 18–30.

Kalev, A., Kelly, E., & Dobbin, F. (2006). Best practices or best guesses? Assessing the efficacy of corporate affirmative action and diversity policies. *American Sociological Review, 71*, 589–617.

Kelly, E., & Dobbin, F. (1998). How affirmative action became diversity management. *American Behavioral Scientist, 41*, 960–984.

Leonard, J. S. (1990). The impact of affirmative action regulation and equal employment law on Black employment. *Journal of Economic Perspectives, 4*, 47–63.

Nilsson, S., & Ellström, P. (2012). Employability and talent management: Challenges for HRD practices. *European Journal of Training and Development, 36*, 26–45.

Thomas, R. R., Jr. (1990). From affirmative action to affirming diversity. *Harvard Business Review, March-April 1990*, 5–15.

CHAPTER 4

TALENT DEVELOPMENT OF REFUGEE WOMEN IN THE UNITED STATES

Minerva D. Tuliao, Katherine M. Najjar, and Richard J. Torraco

In almost all refugee populations approximately half are women (Martin, 2004; UNHCR, 2014). The United Nations High Commissioner for Refugees (UNHCR) describes refugees as individuals who are forced to migrate to other countries due to war, civil unrest, or fears of persecution. Not only do refugees receive no protection from their own government, it is frequently their own country that has threatened their personal security and freedom.

Refugee women face particular challenges when integrating into new communities, especially industrialized countries. Young women may unexpectedly be required to assume the role of caregivers or sole breadwinners when traditional heads of household are unable to learn local languages, or have difficulties adapting to the workforce. Older or single mothers lack the traditional support and friendship networks that extended families provide (Yakushko, 2010). Often unprepared for the new work environment, many refugee women lack sufficient language skills, technological experience, or cultural competence to adequately support a household or

Talent Development and the Global Economy:
Perspectives from Special Interest Groups, pp. 41–60
Copyright © 2017 by Information Age Publishing

even themselves. Past experiences of trauma may exacerbate the difficulties of transition (UNHCR, 2008).

Part of claiming a rightful place in the host countries is full participation in society. Women who are alone or who are heads of household must be assisted with the tools and training that will permit them to acquire housing, transportation, healthcare, and other necessities, with the eventual goal of being fully independent and contributing members of their new communities. Preparing for the workforce through talent development is the first step on their journey of independence and empowerment (Yakushko, Backhaus, Watson, Ngaruiya, & Gonzalez, 2008). In this chapter, we will discuss how potential talent can be identified and developed during the critical stage of pre-employment of refugee women resettling in industrialized countries.

BACKGROUND OF REFUGEES

Refugees are persons who have "a well-founded fear of being persecuted because of race, religion, nationality, membership to a particular social group or political opinion, and unable or, because of such fear, are unwilling to return to that country (United States of America, 2016, p. 1). This definition extends to persons escaping war, other armed conflicts, or generalized violence (UNHCR, 2014). As global climate change becomes more pronounced, UNHCR expects increasing numbers of refugees due to natural disasters (UNCHR, 2008). Prior to entering industrialized countries of asylum such as the United States, most refugees typically spend years at a refugee camp where they are processed for refugee status. Once granted by the government of an industrialized country, refugees are classified as part of the *immigrant* or the *foreign-born* population. If sent to the United States, they may apply for lawful permanent residence or a green card after one year of continuous presence in the United States, and citizenship after 5 years (Lyons, 2008; Nwosu, Batalova, & Auclair, 2014). Aside from refugees, other immigrants include asylees, naturalized citizens, green card holders, persons on temporary visas, and the unauthorized or undocumented.

While refugees are referred to as immigrants, the profile and needs of refugees are distinctly different from the rest of the foreign-born population. Compared to other immigrants, the size of the refugee population is small, but it is considered a vulnerable group because of the hardships they have endured due to war, civil unrest, and forced migration (Brandt, 2010; Wrigley, 2007). Host countries such as the United States with long-established humanitarian programs ensure that refugees receive special assistance in resettlement transitions, which include family reunification, adult English literacy programs linked to employment, job placement services, housing, mental health counseling, medical care, and integration programs (Brandt, 2010; Lyons, 2008; University of Pittsburgh, 2014, Wrigley, 2007). Unlike other types of immigrants, refugees are legally authorized to work in the country upon resettlement, and in the United States are eligible for the same public benefits and services as U.S. citizens (Lyons, 2008).

Refugee Women

At the end of the year 2016, the United States legally admitted about 84,000 refugees (United States Department of State, Bureau of Population, Refugees and Migration, 2016).

Researchers have suggested that refugee arrivals tend to be more women than men from more rural homelands who resettle in urban communities with fewer pre-established community support structures, and refugees are more educationally disadvantaged compared to other types of immigrants (Connor, 2010; Magno, 2008; Wrigley, 2007). Additionally, female refugee arrivals from Africa and the Middle East are single mothers who are more at risk for marginalization in their new country due to having the sole responsibility of childcare and the need to attain self-sufficiency (Magno, 2008). Though the 2011 Office of Refugee Resettlement (ORR) report did not distinguish the education and English proficiency levels between refugee men and women (United States Department of Health and Human Services, 2011), other researchers have suggested that refugee women arrive at their countries of resettlement with varying levels of skill, work experience, and education (Guerin, Guerin, Diirye, & Abdi, 2005; Martin, 2004; Warriner, 2004).

As of 2011, the employment rate for refugee men was 62%, compared to 42% for refugee women. More refugee men also actively looked for work (73%), compared to the women (53%), although it is not clear in the ORR report in what types of jobs or organizations refugee women are employed (United States Department of Health and Human Services, 2011). However, other researchers have determined that if refugees do find employment, they typically work in low-paying, low-status jobs, and are hired often without regard to their human capital, within poor working conditions with little opportunity for career advancement (Bloch, 2009; Colic-Peisker & Tilbury, 2006; Lamba, 2003; Morrice, 2007; Sienkiewicz, Mauceri, Howell, & Bibeau, 2013; Yakushko, 2010). This suggests that economic adjustment can continue to be challenging for refugee populations. Connor (2010) observed that refugees generally had more room for economic progress than other immigrant groups, but only because they entered the U.S. labor market at a much lower occupational level than other immigrant groups.

Despite these conditions, refugee women are found to be resilient, which debunks the stereotype of the poor, failing, and unmotivated immigrant (Warriner, 2004). Many are optimistic and determined to rebuild their lives in their new communities by balancing motherhood, being committed students, and pursuing or resuming their careers (Yakushko, 2006). Many refugee women want to work and become more educated. Regardless of marital status, they understand that employment will lead to improved lives for themselves and their families (Warriner, 2004). This determination is evident in an Australian study of Sudanese refugees conducted by Burgoyne and Hull (2007). Burgoyne and Hull found that despite low levels of English and formal basic education, younger Sudanese refugee women aged 25–44 years old were more eager to enter the workforce in comparison to middle-aged or older women. In order to assist their own and their children's resettlement, the number of women attendees of English classes equally matched that of the men. Clearly, refugee women understand the need for training and education to enhance their language, skills, and therefore their economic positions in their new country (Glastra & Meerman, 2011; Warriner, 2004; Yakushko, 2010). Key to capitalizing on refugee women's commitment as well as identifying potential hidden skills and abilities is talent development.

TALENT IS CRITICAL TO EMPLOYABILITY

Talent is critical to refugees being employable (Nilsson & Ellstrom, 2012). Employability considers the aspects of an individual's human capital and talent including knowledge, skills, abilities, attitudes, and personal characteristics. An individual may possess characteristics marketed as desirable to employers, however these are not necessarily associated with talent, such as formal qualifications and social capital (Hillage & Pollard, 1998; Knight & Yorke, 2004; McQuaid & Lindsay, 2005). Though employability is a complex concept, an individual's formal credentials and degrees are generally considered to be central to individual employability (Nilsson & Ellstrom, 2012). Work experience is also valued by employers and those skills acquired on the job can have a positive impact on future employment prospects (de Vroome & van Tubergen, 2010).

Finding ways in which talent, training, and skillsets can be identified, expressed, and developed is important at all stages of an individual's work life, but this task is especially crucial in the pre-employment stage. Talent is often perceived as an individual characteristic based on a socially acceptable and restricted set of characteristics and behaviors in situated contexts

(Barab & Plucker, 2002; Glastra & Meerman, 2012). For talent to be identified, expressed, and developed in refugee women, they must be given the opportunity to build and strengthen both human and social capital. At the pre-employment stage, human capital such as knowledge, skills, and experience can be identified, expressed, and developed through pre-employment educational and training opportunities. Further, newcomers who achieve academic qualifications still face a disadvantage if they do not also have the appropriate social capital (Morrice, 2007). Opportunities to build "bridging" or "linking" social capital (Putnam, 2000) must also be identified, expressed, and developed at the pre-employment stage, which will enable them to learn, access information, and gain advantage from extended connections and relationships built outside their own social milieu.

Accessing the workforce in one's first job is a challenge for all workers—citizens and migrants alike. The ability to communicate and display relevant skills for the workplace is crucial to employability and the transition to employment.

TALENT DEVELOPMENT AT THE PRE-EMPLOYMENT STAGE

Upon arrival in the industrialized country of resettlement, refugee women who wish to find employment are typically assisted by resettlement agencies in education, training, and integration. This section describes the skills that refugee women bring with them to resettling countries or may gain from learning experiences during the resettlement and pre-employment stages, and demonstrates how the development of talent can occur at the pre-employment stage.

Job Skills and English Language Literacy

As an initial step toward career advancement, refugee women are assisted in finding opportunities for pre-employment training. This includes short-term training such as vocational training, on-the-job-training, or job clubs. For example, some discretionary assistance programs offer short-term vocational skill training for 3 to 4 months in a certified skill (Halpern, 2008). Some agencies may also have a "job club" where refugees can practice writing resumes and job applications.

Pre-employment training also includes English-as-a-second-language (ESL) training, with a particular emphasis on employment-related English (Halpern, 2008). ESL classes are largely offered by independent nonprofit organizations and community colleges (Martin, 2004). Though some nonprofit community organizations offer free English language literacy training, it can be costly to study for skills recertification, earn a high school diploma or its equivalent (GED), attend higher education, or pursue other forms of adult education (Cultural Orientation Resource Center, 2012). Some pre-employment education programs also include financial literacy, where refugees learn basic skills as debit card usage, as well as more advanced skills such as maintaining credit in the context of the United States financial system (Halpern, 2008). Most of these educational programs have monthly tests that assess various competencies to see whether students are ready for employment (Elkin, Barden, & Mueller, 2008).

In a study by Koyama (2013), a Somali woman refugee was identified for her ability to learn English very quickly while undergoing English language training at a refugee camp. Her instructor recognized this skill and set her aside for further language tutoring. By the time she arrived in the United States to resettle, her English was good enough to help her ease into workforce training activities and find work. Despite the challenging conditions of being a widow and a single mother, living in poverty, and having no long-term formal education, this case exemplifies the identification and development of potential talent in the stages prior to securing employment. The ability to learn, adapt, and utilize self-efficacy are precisely the types of talent that individuals who are working with refugees need to focus on and, if possible, cultivate.

Life Skills

In addition to offering English literacy and vocational training, some nonprofit community organizations also provide refugees cultural orientation, and nonformal and practical life skills education (Magno, 2008; Shriberg, Downs-Karkos, & Weisberg, 2012; Suleman & Whiteford, 2013). Such community organizations help refugees learn how to navigate local systems of education and employment, and discuss relevant issues of tenancy, healthcare, maternal literacy and childcare, transportation, and financial services. For refugee women especially, such settings encourage the social networking needed to bring them together to learn informally from each other, communicate their needs, or help them find employment (Butterwick, 2003; Lyytinen & Kullenberg, 2013; Magno, 2008; Shriberg, et al., 2012; Suleman & Whiteford, 2013). Because this knowledge helps to build a refugee's confidence in engaging in her environment, such learning opportunities are believed to be critical in resettlement transitions and integral to occupational engagement and well-being (Suleman & Whiteford, 2013).

In such nonformal settings, refugee women are already undergoing learning activities that could build on current strengths and develop potential talent. For instance, one such community organization encourages refugee women to participate in the organization's community activities to help them learn critical knowledge and skills that they would otherwise not obtain through formal education (Magno, 2008). Some of these knowledge and skills include computer and typing skills, public speaking, and budgeting. By interacting with other women of varied cultures, nationalities, and backgrounds, they are encouraged to practice their English communication skills and broaden their understanding of different cultures. In addition, forming relationships across cultures improves their opportunities for workforce success. By connecting with others, they are able to form a peer network or support group. Ties with local individuals or other immigrants are found to be valuable in refugees' motivation for adaptation (de Vroome & van Tubergen, 2010; Sienkiewicz et al., 2013).

CHALLENGES TO THE TALENT DEVELOPMENT OF REFUGEE WOMEN

It is clear that potential talent can be developed by building on current skills and strengths refugee women bring with them upon arrival, or can be encouraged through job skill training and life skills education by participating in learning opportunities prior to employment. However, a number of issues remain as to why some of these programs may not be conducive in the identification and development of women refugee talent at the pre-employment stage.

Program Access, Quality, and Cultural Barriers

In order to build on strengths and for potential talent to emerge, programs for refugee women must be sensitive to their needs and meet the conditions for facilitative and meaningful learning. Many workforce development programs focus on male-dominated jobs (Manery & Cohen, 2003; Martin, 2004). Martin (2004) found that thus far development-oriented efforts for refugee participants have been focused on refugee men. This is because many of the projects designed to promote community development consisted of large-scale construction and reforestation schemes, which primarily involve employing refugee men. Development-oriented projects and programs in countries of asylum and resettlement are believed to enhance refugee economic independence, reduce the host country's refugee assistance costs, and facilitate returns traditionally through infrastructure improvement (Martin, 2004).

Even if training programs are available, refugee women may not be able to access them due to issues with childcare, transportation, family responsibilities, and cultural barriers (Davison, 1981). The provision of transportation and childcare services on site can help increase the participation of refugee women in training, education, and employment. Some educational classes were found to be not culturally sensitive for refugee women (Davison, 1981). Educational classes that combine men and women together in the same room may discourage refugee women from attending and participating in classes. In attending mixed classes, some refugee women claim to be afraid that men would lose face if the women did better, and other women professed shyness in such classes. In addition, some refugee women preferred to participate in learning sessions that were held in informal settings versus formally organized classes. This was because formal classes required them to seek approval from their husbands and were perceived to be threatening to cultural beliefs about family unity and male authority.

Furthermore, literacy programs do not sufficiently assess individual learning and progression levels due to lack of resources (Clayton, 2005; Elkin et al., 2008). Some refugee women with intermediate English skills have expressed frustrations at being placed, by default, in the same classrooms as those who were just learning the English alphabet (Clayton, 2005).

Unrealistic Timelines to Employment

In the United States, refugees have an average of 90 days to find employment (Halpern, 2008; Warriner, 2004). Within this period, refugees are on welfare and receive assistance to learn English, get job skills training, and find jobs. Beyond the average 90-day period, refugees risk losing welfare assistance, thus securing paid employment is prioritized over learning English and other skills integral for long-term self-sufficiency (Dunman, 2006; Elkin et al., 2008; Sienkewicz et al., 2013). This timeline is unrealistic for anyone, but especially so for refugee women who are single parents, have limited financial and social support for childcare, lack transportation to participate in classes, have less formal education than men, and have lower levels of English proficiency (Martin, 2004; Spero, 1985; Warriner, 2004). In their study on Sudanese refugee women resettling in Australia, Burgoyne and Hull (2007) found that those with a low basic formal education and limited English needed more time to develop learning skills, and skills in speaking, reading, and writing English. Because of family responsibilities, which often include caring for many children, and/or being the sole breadwinners, refugees women were often too overfatigued to learn. Many immigrants and refugees have reported feelings of exhaustion because of the challenges of working multiple jobs and learning the language and culture while struggling with family responsibilities (Yakushko, 2010).

Lack of Workforce Development Program Integration

In addition to the unrealistic 90-day timeline, there are very few programs that integrate English language skills with contextualized job skills training (Moran & Petsod, 2003). It is assumed that employers will provide the necessary training once refugee women are employed, but it is also rare for employers to invest in basic skills training such as reading, writing, math, and English proficiency in the workplace (Moran & Petsod, 2003; Yakushko et al., 2008). Koyama (2013) quoted several managers who did not believe improving language skills was in an employer's best interest. "Several managers concurred and candidly identified the greatest risk in hiring refugees as the possibility that once they learned more English, the refugees would find more challenging, higher-paid positions" (Koyama, 2013, p. 958). Balancing the best interests of both workers and employers may prove to be a long-term challenge.

Researchers have demonstrated that cultural orientation classes are not mandated nor consistently integrated with pre-employment programs for refugees. Cultural orientation classes discuss topics such as work norms, barriers to finding gainful employment in their country of resettlement, and the current economy (de Vroome & van Tubergen, 2010; Sienkewicz et al., 2013). If refugees do attend cultural orientation, these classes are not offered regularly, vary in program length, and should be reviewed to include topics that better prepare refugees for life in the country, such as positive coping strategies in dealing with stressors related to job seeking and employment identity (Sienkewicz et al., 2013).

In fleeing war and civil unrest in their home countries, many of these women have also experienced violent traumatic events. Researchers have found that refugees who experienced violent traumatic events prior to resettlement were less motivated to learn a foreign language compared to other immigrants who voluntarily left their home countries (Iversen, Sveaass, & Morken, 2012). The opportunity for refugees to learn coping strategies enough to be motivated to learn English, in addition to learning skills for employability and adjusting to a new country, could take more than 3 months to accomplish. Benseman (2014) noted that refugee learning is variable and it may take as long as 4 to 5 years just to learn survival English. However, they leave English classes because of the pressure to find jobs.

To date, there is little research on the integration of mental health and trauma counseling in current skill development programming for refugees. Because the motivation to learn a new language is affected by past traumatic experiences, and language learning is key to employability, psychosocial support programs should also be integrated in resettlement assistance and workforce development programs (Cardozo, Talley, Burton, & Crawford, 2004; Iversen et al., 2014). Doing so could increase self-efficacy, which is linked to newcomers' perceptions of their success. Self-efficacy may be developed and reinforced through career and behavioral counseling (Yakushko et al., 2008). Similarly, Suleman and Whiteford (2013) noted the potential value of what they called "tenacity skills" (p. 206). Although self-efficacy is not a trait that individuals possess in equal measure, fostering feelings of success and competence is important to mental and emotional health, as well as economic achievement (Yakushko, 2010). Identifying evidence of self-efficacy and bringing that evidence forward as a talent to be developed is one way to recognize an individual's abilities.

Nonrecognition of Current Skills and Qualifications

The nonrecognition of the current skills and qualifications of refugees as major barriers to employability and career advancement is well-documented. Often times, employers do not recognize the refugees' work experience and education that they received from their home countries. Refugees who have earned professional degrees in their home countries often end up in jobs that they are overqualified for, thus rendering them underemployed or needing to be retrained for what is accepted as "relevant" work experience and formal qualifications (Bloch, 2009; Colic-Peisker & Tilbury, 2006; Glastra & Meerman, 2012; Lamba, 2003; Tomlinson & Egan, 2002). In their originating countries, many refugee women may have worked in mostly rural or agricultural jobs, skills that may not be perceived as transferrable to jobs in urban, industrialized environments (Spero, 1985). Thus, these women need to retrain for new jobs, or risk working in low-paying, low-skilled jobs with little to no advancement, or not being offered a job at all.

Refugee women bring many skills with them before they arrive at their country of resettlement. In a study on Somali refugee women resettling in New Zealand, Guerin et al. (2005) found that these refugee women possessed a diverse set of skills and work experience gained from Somalia. Some had been self-employed and had their own small businesses, from owning and operating reputable establishments such as restaurants or clothing stores, to trading dry foods and farming. Others had professional careers as nurses and factory workers. These prior work experiences reflect varied skills and talents in business and financial management, marketing, and healthcare, as well as skills in negotiation, social networking, and knowledge of regional-specific trades, to name a few (Guerin et al., p. 45). Upon arriving in New Zealand, these refugee women were concerned about their lack of fluency in formal and informal settings in which they could demonstrate their social and communication skills. If they were to resume the same work in their country of resettlement, current programs would need to acknowledge the prior work experiences and skills obtained from their origin countries.

RECOMMENDATIONS

The following recommendations attempt to address the challenges associated with the development of talent in refugee women during the pre-employment stage. They include the utilization of the nonprofit community organization and its partners as a source of holistic and integrated learning and development, developing strategies to identify and recognize prior skills and talent, and developing the refugee woman's current skillsets for self-employment.

The Nonprofit Community Sector and Its Partners

The nonprofit sector is increasingly taking on the lion's share in addressing needs associated with integrated learning experiences. These nonprofit organizations partner with businesses and community colleges in providing vocational English in the context of building skills that employers need, as well as place refugee program participants in the talent pipeline for future job opportunities with employers (Moran & Petsod, 2003). In addition, nonprofit community centers in the United States and Canada that are run by and for immigrant and refugee women increasingly provide a more holistic, integrated approach to skills development (Manery & Cohen, 2003). These training programs combine employment-related English language instruction, job training, job services, work experience, and life skills training. Community-based programs with a holistic approach to skill development are said to be more effective because they are more responsive to women's needs and goals in improving employability (Manery & Cohen, 2003). In addition, work experiences through community organization activities, if recognized as informal on-the-job experiences, enable refugee women to demonstrate and build various skills, such as communicating in English and social networking (Magno, 2008; Manery & Cohen, 2003). Such conditions of integrated and holistic learning experiences can provide a rich avenue for identification, recognition, and development of potential talent and strengths of refugee women.

Integrate Mentoring With Education and Training

Aside from including refugee women in the talent pipeline, employers who partner with nonprofit community organizations can also help refugee women with their transition to employment by matching them with mentors from the organization. Research shows that refugee women who receive mentoring by local or native-born working women, in combination with life skills education, cultural orientation, and pre-employment job skill development, fare better in terms of their transition to employment (Burgoyne & Hull, 2007; Dennett, 2008; Manery & Cohen, 2003). In matching a refugee's career goals with a mentor's professional expertise, age, gender, and regional proximity, the mentor can guide the refugee with (a) work issues, such as work norms and culture, resume writing, computer skills, resources for education and training, and expand the refugee's network of friends and professional associates; and (b) practical life issues (such as teaching how to pay the bills, take public transportation, etc.), awareness of societal and cultural norms, and general support and understanding of refugees' experiences in rebuilding lives, finding employment, or advancing their careers (Dennett, 2008). Forming developmental relationships such as mentoring, providing psycho-social support, and career advising, is a type of talent development strategy that aims to help talented individuals understand big picture issues and see new perspectives (Garavan, Carbery, & Rock, 2011). In this relationship, the mentor's role can also be that of someone who can identify refugee strengths and talent, encourage these talents to be developed during the pre-employment stage, and recommend potential jobs where talents can be recognized and further developed. It can also be implied that a developmental relationship is a type of social capital, such that the relationship enables a refugee woman to extend her professional network and learn from a mentor who has a similar work environment. Though mentorship is said to be beneficial to refugee resettlement and pre-employment transitions, such arrangements are rare as they are only sometimes a part of volunteer and advocacy programs of employer and nonprofit partnerships (Dennett, 2008).

Integrate Counseling With Education and Training

It is also evident that psychosocial well-being and self-efficacy is critical to refugee women as they adjust to new lives and transition to employment.

Though trauma counseling is provided by resettlement agencies, research suggests that counseling and psycho-social support programs may not be well-integrated with other refugee programs that aim to improve employability (Iversen et al., 2014; Cardozo et al., 2004).

Strategies to Identify and Recognize Talent

Before talent can be developed, it first has to identified and recognized. To date, there is growing interest in innovative strategies that refugee women, adult educators, career counselors, and potential employers can participate in order to reveal hidden talent, make these recognizable, and thus have the potential to be developed.

Educate the Educator

Educators of adult refugees are often the first to interact with refugee women during the pre-employment stage thus making these educators instrumental in the talent development of refugee women. However, most of these educators are volunteers of community organizations who service refugees and who may have little professional experience in adult learning, varied and effective teaching methods, work with interpreters, and teach non-English speakers (Perry & Hart, 2012; Tuomi, 2005). Due to the often limited funding of community organizations in providing training for these educators of adult refugees, most educators rely on self-directed learning by reading professional books, utilizing the Internet for teaching and learning resources, asking experts for advice, and observing and reflecting on teaching experiences. Benseman (2014) conducted a study in New Zealand and found that bilingual tutors are most effective, and that refugee educators in general needed greater access to cross-cultural sensitivity training and translated material to support instructional preparation and delivery. If educators of adult refugees received more support for such professional development, they may become more skilled in identifying and recognizing students' strengths, skills, and talents during their teaching experiences, which might enable them to further nurture these strengths through a variety of meaningful learning experiences.

The Importance of Life Skills

In the United Kingdom, the "life curriculum vitae" or life CV has been used with refugees to support conventional, westernized CVs where only formal education is listed (Schultheiss, Watts, Sterland, & O'Neill, 2011). Through a story-telling process, the life CV tells (a) the experiences of the refugee; (b) enables them to expose talents, skills, and abilities that would otherwise be overlooked if the focus was on the formal education typically required; and (c) highlights how these experiences can be used in the job market. The study finds that through this process many strengths are revealed, such as coping strategies, resiliency, skills, knowledge, qualifications, support networks, and values. The life CV has also been found to reduce negative attitudes in the recruitment and development process that may undermine skills, knowledge, and self-efficacy that typically results in talents remaining hidden, unrecognized, and disrupting identity. Such a process can be used to advocate alternative practices as a means of demonstrating potential talent for development and employability. The importance of considering life experiences when evaluating the skillsets of migrants has also been noted in other studies (Suleman & Whiteford, 2013; Werquin, 2012).

Emphasize the Recognition of Prior Learning

Another consideration is the use of services and assessments dedicated to recognizing refugees' human capital. These are formal skills and qualifications obtained overseas, or for those lacking such formal credentials, the recognition of prior learning, skills, and experience. In Scotland, a study explored the need for dedicated recognition services—or recognition of prior learning (RPL)—as a response to an increasing number of migrant workers and refugees in that country (Guest & Vecchia, 2010). It was found that many education and training providers and employers were already using some form of recognition of prior skills and qualifications, albeit with different definitions. Thus, there is a need for a common, easily identifiable approach to the recognition of skills, learning, and qualifications, as well as the transferability of these skills, to support refugee access to relevant education, training, and employment. At present, relevant stakeholders in Scotland are collaborating to develop an RPL toolkit that includes information on assessing, documenting, and recording previous learning and skills, which can be used by education and training providers, employers, and human resource personnel (Guest & Vecchia, 2010; Werquin, 2012).

Self-Identification of Talent Potential

Career counselors can help refugee women in the self-identification of talent and potential. Yakushko et al. (2008) highlighted the importance of working with newcomers to facilitate adjustment, social network development, and language skills. Using the social cognitive career theory, they noted that the context of an individual's life experiences influenced both career choices and opportunities; career advisers and counselors may need to help clients to reframe a trait (such as having an accent) as an indication of adaptability, intelligence, and resilience.

Building on Current Skillsets for Self-Employment

If being employed by an organization is not an option for personal or cultural reasons, self-employment may be an alternative choice. As discussed earlier, many refugee women arrive with limited formal schooling, limited English, and less formal credentials compared to men. But it is possible that they have skills learned as they go through their daily lives or previous work experiences, which may be perceived as strengths and potential talents to be developed. For instance, recent arrivals of Karenni refugee women from Burma have leveraged their current skills in traditional weaving and basket making into the means of a livelihood in Utah (Stephenson, Smith, Gibson, & Watson, 2013). In addition, many refugee women volunteer in the activities of nonprofit community organizations. Skills from these nonformal and informal learning experiences may be assessed given the opportunity to demonstrate them in such settings.

Currently, there are a few nonprofit community organizations that help develop the talents of refugee women and migrants in microenterprise. Aside from handicrafts, other small businesses include food preparation, tailoring, and caregiving for adults or children. Although women who have low levels of education may need support through explanation of laws and regulations, taxes and bookkeeping, and continuing education, entrepreneurialism may be a way for women to develop independence, creativity, and self-efficacy. Microlending may be a particularly promising vehicle for new business development. Its use as an economic tool, particularly for women, has been well-documented (Yunus, 2008)

FUTURE TRENDS

We can expect to see continual inflows of refugee women at all skill levels and continued efforts to successfully integrate them into society and productive lives. Although much attention is placed upon regions of the world in crisis, individuals are displaced and flee from their countries for a variety of reasons. As the global climate changes, future crises will be related to famine, riparian or coastal flooding, and drought (UNHCR, 2008). How communities and businesses bring newcomers into the economy will be vital to the social stability and economic well-being of all citizens.

CONCLUSION

Talent development is a process wherein the pre-employment stage holds great potential for the identification and development of strengths and talents. This is particularly true when communities are seeking to successfully integrate vulnerable groups like refugee women into society. Gender roles, trauma, educational background, and family responsibility disproportionately affect these women. Community support for the investment in adult education in nonprofit sectors, microbusiness incubators, integrated workforce development programs, and social support networks all have the potential to develop the talents of refugee women and create their successful transition into the workforce and society. The efforts of many industrialized countries are noted, but much more work needs to be done for meaningful and sustainable socioeconomic development.

REFERENCES

Barab, S. A., & Plucker, J. A. (2002). Smart people or smart contexts? Cognition, ability, and talent development in an age of situated approaches to knowing and learning. *Educational Psychologist, 37*(3), 165–182.

Benseman, J. (2014). Adult refugee learners with limited literacy: Needs and effective responses. *Refuge, 3*(1), 93–103.

Bloch, A. (2009). Barriers to the labour market: Refugees in Britain. In S. McKay (Ed.), *Refugees, recent migrants and employment: Challenging barriers and exploring pathways* (pp. 165–183). New York, NY: Routledge.

Brandt, K. (2010). *Making immigrant integration work: A case study of refugee resettlement in Philadelphia*. Unpublished master's thesis, Iowa State University, Ames, IA.

Burgoyne, U., & Hull, O. (2007). Classroom management strategies to address the needs of Sudanese refugee learners: Support document—methodology and literature review. Adelaide, South Australia: *National Centre for Vocational Education Research*.

Butterwick, S. (2003). Life skills training: Open for discussion. In M. G. Cohen (Ed.), *Training the excluded for work: Access and equity for women, immigrants, first nations, youth, and people with low income* (pp. 161–177). Vancouver, BC, Canada: UBC Press.

Cardozo, B. L., Talley, L., Burton, A., & Crawford, C. (2004). Karenni refugees living in Thai–Burmese border camps: Traumatic experiences, mental health outcomes, and social functioning. *Social Science & Medicine, 58*(12), 2637–2644.

Clayton, P. (2005). Blank slates or hidden treasure? Assessing and building on the experiential learning of migrant and refugee women in European countries. *International Journal of Lifelong Education*, *24*(3), 227–242.

Colic-Peisker, V., & Tilbury, F. (2006). Employment niches for recent refugees: Segmented labour market in twenty-first century Australia. *Journal of Refugee Studies*, *19*(2), 203–229.

Connor, P. (2010). Explaining the refugee gap: Economic outcomes of refugees versus other immigrants. *Journal of Refugee Studies*, *23*(3), 377–397.

Cultural Orientation Resource Center, Center for Applied Linguistics. (2012). *Welcome to the United States: A guidebook for refugees* (4th ed). Washington, DC: Author. Retrieved from http://www.culturalorientation.net/content/download/2185/12569/version/1/file/2012-English-Welcome_Guide.pdf

Davison, L. (1981). Refugee women: Special needs and programs. *Journal of Refugee Resettlement*, *1*(3), 16–26.

Dennett, R. (2008). Taking the next step: The importance of mentoring. *Migration Action*, (1), 16.

de Vroome, T., & van Tubergen, F. (2010). The employment experiences of refugees in the Netherlands. *International Migration Review*, *44*(2), 376–403.

Dunman, K. M. (2006). *Improving long-term resettlement services for refugees, asylees, and asylum seekers: Perspectives from service providers* (Masters thesis). University of South Florida. Retrieved from http://scholarcommons.usf.edu/cgi/viewcontent.cgi?article=3510&context=etd

Elkin, S., Barden, B., & Mueller, M. (2008). *The evaluation of the refugee social service (RSS) and targeted assistance formula grant (TAG) programs: Sacramento case study*. Washington DC: United States Department of Health and Human Services. Retrieved from http://www.acf.hhs.gov/sites/default/files/orr/sacramentocasestudy.pdf

Garavan, T. N., Carbery, R., & Rock, A. (2012). Mapping talent development: Definition, scope and architecture. *European Journal of Training and Development*, *36*(1), 5–24.

Glastra, F. J., & Meerman, M. (2012). Developing ethnic talent in the Dutch national tax administration: A case study. *European Journal of Training and Development*, *36*(1), 105–124.

Guerin, B., Guerin, P., Diirye, R. O., & Abdi, A. (2005). What skills do Somali refugees bring with them? *New Zealand Journal of Employment Relations*, *30*(2), 37–49.

Guest, P., & Vecchia, M. (2010). *Scoping study on support mechanisms for the recognition of the skills, learning, and qualifications of migrant workers and refugees: Final report*. Glasgow, Scotland: Scottish Credit and Qualifications Framework Partnership.

Halpern, P. (2008). *Refugee economic self-sufficiency: An exploratory study of approaches used in Office of Refugee Resettlement programs*. Washington DC: United States Department of Health and Human Services. Retrieved from http://aspe.hhs.gov/hsp/08/RefugeeSelfSuff/report.pdf

Hillage, J., & Pollard, E. (1998). *Employability: Developing a framework for policy analysis*. London, England: Department for Education and Employment.

Iversen, V. C., Sveaass, N., & Morken, G. (2014). The role of trauma and psychological distress on motivation for foreign language acquisition among refugees. *International Journal of Culture and Mental Health, 7*(1), 59–67.

Knight, P., & Yorke, M. (2004). *Learning, curriculum and employability in higher education.* London, England: Routledge.

Koyama, J. (2013). Resettling notions of social mobility: Locating refugees as 'educable' and 'employable.' *British Journal of Sociology of Education, 34*(5/6), 947–965.

Lamba, N. K. (2003). The employment experiences of Canadian refugees: Measuring the impact of human and social capital on quality of employment. *Canadian Review of Sociology, 40*(1), 45–64.

Lyons, C. (2008). Differentiating between refugees and immigrants: Two sets of challenges. In *Navigating government immigration issues: Leading immigration and refugee resettlement experts on addressing employment, education, and health care issues for immigrants* (pp. 7–20). Eagan, MN: Thomson/Aspatore.

Lyytinen, E., & Kullenberg, J. (2013). *An analytical report: Urban refugee research.* New York, NY: Women's Refugee Commission. Retrieved from http://www.womensrefugeecommission.org/joomlatools-files/docman-files/Urban_Refugee_Research_Analytical_Report_-_February_2013.pdf

Magno, C. (2008). Refuge from crisis: Refugee women build political capital. *Globalisation, Societies and Education, 6*(2), 119–130.

Manery, M., & Cohen, M. G. (2003). Community skills training by and for immigrant women. In M. G. Cohen (Ed.), *Training the excluded for work: Access and equity for women, immigrants, first nations, youth, and people with low income* (pp. 145–160). Vancouver, BC, Canada: UBC Press.

Martin, S. F. (2004). *Refugee women* (2nd ed.). Lanham, MD: Lexington Books.

McQuaid, R. W., & Lindsay, C. (2005). The concept of employability. *Urban Studies, 42*(2), 197–219.

Moran, T., & Petsod, D. (2003). *Newcomers in the American workplace: Improving employment outcomes for low-wage immigrants and refugees.* New York, NY: Rockefeller Foundation.

Morrice, L. (2007). Lifelong learning and the social integration of refugees in the UK: The significance of social capital. *International Journal of Lifelong Education, 26*(2), 155–172.

Nilsson, S., & Ellström, P. E. (2012). Employability and talent management: Challenges for HRD practices. *European Journal of Training and Development, 36*(1), 26–45.

Nwosu, C., Batalova, J., & Auclair, G. (2014, April 28). Frequently requested statistics on immigrants and immigration in the United States. *Migration Policy Institute.* Retrieved from http://www.migrationpolicy.org/article/frequently-requested-statistics-immigrants-and-immigration-united-states

Perry, K. H., & Hart, S. J. (2012). "I'm just kind of winging it": Preparing and supporting educators of adult refugee learners. *Journal of Adolescent & Adult Literacy, 56*(2), 110–122.

Putnam, R.D. (2000). *Bowling alone: The collapse and revival of American community.* New York, NY: Simon and Schuster.

Schultheiss, D. E., Watts, J., Sterland, L., & O'Neill, M. (2011). Career, migration and the life CV: A relational cultural analysis. *Journal of Vocational Behavior, 78*, 334–341.

Shriberg, J., Downs-Karkos, S., & Weisberg, S. (2012). Non-formal education as a means of supporting the well-being of resettled refugees: Case studies of community approaches in Denver, Colorado. In L. Demirdjian (Ed.), *Education as a humanitarian response: Education, refugees, and asylum seekers* (pp. 131–150). New York, NY: Continuum.

Sienkiewicz, H. C., Mauceri, K. G., Howell, E. C., & Bibeau, D. L. (2013). Untapped resources: Refugee employment experiences in central North Carolina. *Work, 45*, 17–24.

Spero, A. (1985). *In America and in need: Immigrant, refugee, and entrant women*. Washington, DC: American Association of Community and Junior Colleges.

Stephenson, S. M., Smith, Y. J., Gibson, M., & Watson, V. (2013). Traditional weaving as an occupation of Karen refugee women. *Journal of Occupational Science, 20*(3), 224–235.

Suleman, A. S. & Whiteford, G. E. (2013). Understanding occupational transitions in forced migration: The importance of life skills in early refugee resettlement. *Journal of Occupational Science, 20*(2), 201–210.

Tomlinson, F., & Egan, S. (2002). From marginalization to (dis)empowerment: Organizing training and employment services for refugees. *Human Relations, 55*(8), 1019–1043.

Tuomi, M. T. (2005). Agents of social change in education. *Community Development Journal, 40*(2), 205–211.

United Nations High Commissioner for Refugees. (2008). *UNHCR handbook for the protection of women and girls*. Geneva, Switzerland: Author. Retrieved from http://www.unhcr.org/47cfa9fe2.html

United Nations High Commissioner for Refugees. (2014). *UNHCR global trends*. Geneva, Switzerland: Author. Retrieved from http://www.unhcr.org/556725e69.html#_ga=1.209212820.707237058.1465571786

United States Department of Health and Human Services. (2011). *Report to congress, FY 2011*. Washington D.C.: Office of Refugee Resettlement. Retrieved from https://www.acf.hhs.gov/sites/default/files/orr/fy_2011_orr_annual_report.pdf

United States Department of State, Bureau of Population, Refugees and Migration (2016), *Refugee admissions report*. Retrieved from http://www.wrapsnet.org/admissions-and-arrivals/

United States of America for United Nations High Commissioner for Refugees. (2016). *What is a refugee*. Retrieved from http://www.unrefugees.org/what-is-a-refugee/

University of Pittsburgh. (2014). *Keep it real: Refugee facts*. Retrieved from http://www.pitt.edu/~sorc/keepitreal/RefugeeFacts.html

Warriner, D. (2004). "The days now is very hard for my family": The negotiation and construction of gendered work identities among newly arrived refugee women. *Journal of Language, Identity, and Education, 3*(4), 279–294.

Werquin, P. (2012). The missing link to connect education and employment: Recognition of nonformal and informal learning outcomes. *Journal of Education and Work, 25*(3). 259–278.

Wrigley, H. (2007). Beyond the lifeboat: Improving language, citizenship, and training services for immigrants and refugees. In A. Belzer (Ed.), *Toward defining and improving quality in adult basic education: Issues and challenges* (pp. 221–239). Mahwah, NJ: Lawrence Erlbaum Associates.

Yakushko, O. (2006). Career concerns of immigrant women. In W. B. Walsh & M. J. Heppner (Eds.), *Handbook of career counseling for women* (2nd ed., pp. 387–425). Mahwah, NJ: Lawrence Erlbaum.

Yakushko, O. (2010). Stress and coping strategies in the lives of recent immigrants: A grounded theory model. *International Journal of Advances in Counseling, 32,* 256–273.

Yakushko, O., Backhaus, A., Watson, M., Ngaruiya, K., & Gonzalez, J. (2008). Career development concerns of recent immigrants and refugees. *Journal of Career Development, 34*(4), 362–396.

Yunus, M. (2008). *Creating a world without poverty: Social business and the future of capitalism.* New York, NY: Public Affairs.

CHAPTER 5

THE PRESENCE AND SKILL CIRCULATION OF ASIAN AMERICANS

Hae Na Kim and Yun-Hsiang Hsu

Asians are expected to comprise 5.6% of the U.S. labor force by 2018; in 2010 the U.S. labor force included 7.2 million people of Asian descent (U.S. Department of Labor, 2011). Given this small number, this group of the population demonstrates a relatively high concentration of the graduates who possess diplomas in the professional and tech fields. In 2011, Asian Americans accounted for 14.5% of the science, technology, engineering, and mathematics (STEM) workforce, compared to those in the non-STEM workforce (4.6%, see Figure 5.1). In specific sectors and regions, like the high-tech industry in the Bay Area, the dominance of the Asian population in the workforce is more obvious. The percentage of Asian tech workers was more than 50% in 2010 for this region (Barak, 2012). This is not surprising if there is a closer examination of the number of Asian students who majored in STEM field. According to the American Community Survey, 43% of Asian college students aged 25 and older graduated with STEM majors in 2009 (Beede et al., 2011). In the STEM field, Asian Americans are concentrated on mathematics, natural science, and computer science, while their numbers have increased more broadly in STEM areas (Au, 2007).

Talent Development and the Global Economy:
Perspectives from Special Interest Groups, pp. 61–74
Copyright © 2017 by Information Age Publishing

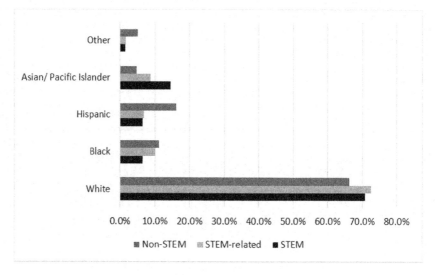

Source: U.S. Census Bureau, 2011 American Community Survey (see www.acs.census.gov/acs).

Figure 5.1.   Percentage Distribution of Students in STEM Programs by Ethnicity.

It seems that the pipeline between professional programs and the labor market for Asian Americans is well constructed; however, their transition is actually not so smooth. The unemployment rate among Asian scientists and engineers is higher than average (Table 5.1), which means that they tend to be underrepresented in the labor market. Even if they make this transition, the career prospects for Asian Americans are dimmer than for mainstream Whites. For example, White males had a 150% advantage over their Asian counterparts when it came to advancement into a managerial level in Silicon Valley's companies (Gee, Peck, & Wong, 2015). The invisible glass ceiling is often cited as the major barrier in the pipeline,[1] which provides an incentive for these highly skilled to return to the countries of their parents or family, such as South Korea, Taiwan, and India, to seek career opportunities. More often than not, these returns are not in a one-way direction because their professional or family connections remain in the United States (Saxenian, 2005; Varrel, 2011). These highly skilled Asian Americans circulate between their mother countries and the United States building a global and professional community based on their ethnic origin.

Asian Americans are a relatively lower percentage when in higher positions. Asian Americans who are in professional positions share 27.2% and managers executives indicate 13.9 %. In addition, only 13.9% of Asian Americans are executives (see Figure 5.2).

**Table 5.1.   Unemployment Rates Among Scientists and
Engineers by Ethnicity: 2013**

Race, Ethnicity, and Sex	Percent
General population	8.1
All scientists and engineers	3.8
White women	3.0
White men	3.4
Asian women	5.9
Asian men	3.2
URM* women	5.6
URM* men	5.7

*URM = underrepresented minority. NOTE: The general population consists of the U.S. civilian noninstitutional population 16 years and over. SOURCE: National Science Foundation, National Center for Science and Engineering Statistics, Scientists and Engineers Statistical Data System (SESTAT), 2013 (preliminary), and Bureau of Labor Statistics, Current Population Survey, 2013.

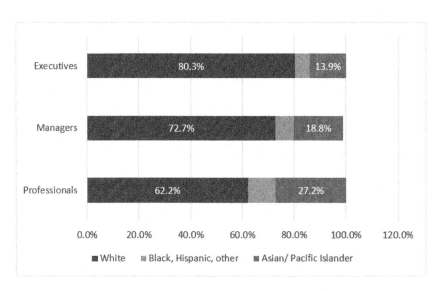

Source: Source: Gee et al. (2015).

Figure 5.2.   Percentage Distribution of Persons in Each Rank by Ethnicity: 2013

These seemingly contradictory facts—overrepresentation of Asian Americans in the student body of professional programs and under-representation in the manager/executive positions at companies—have attracted academic interests who investigate the factors behind it. Tradi-tionally, these issues are viewed from separate academic angles, such as professional education and skill migration. With regard to human resource development (HRD) literature, Asia Americans have not been targeted, although some researchers have focused on the original countries of Asia Pacific Islanders in terms of national human resources development (e.g., Lynham & Cunningham, 2006; McLean, 2004). In this chapter, I will focus on the talent development of Asian American[2] professionals and the tech workforce. I will specifically look into how cultural values shape career choices among Asian youth. I start from a discussion of the cultural conformity on Asian youth's choice of profession, then to the dilemma of a glass ceiling they face in the workplace, and finally to the creation of transnational ethnic professional communities. Policy recommendations are provided after this analysis.

CULTURE CONFORMITY AND OVERREPRESENTATION OF ASIAN AMERICAN IN PROFESSIONAL PROGRAMS

A cultural phenomenon among Asian Americans is the concentration of human power in all professional and technical trades. This can be tracked back to the choice of a school major or graduate program this group has made. Researchers confirmed that Asian parents express expectations about working for stereotypical jobs (Loo, 2005; Fouad et al., 2008; Kim, 2013). This indicates that Asian American families expect to push or rush their children into these trades. One paragraph from Amy Chua's *Battle Hymn of the Tiger Mother*, a book detailing the parenting style of an Asian mother, captures this spirit:

> But Amy, let me ask you this. Who are you doing all this pushing for—your daughters, or—and here always, the cocked head, the knowing tone—or *yourself?* (Chua, 2011)

This population demonstrates conformity to the perceived norm that required decent job and achieve social status when making program or major school decisions. However, Sue and Okazaki (1990) proposed expla-nations other than cultural values. Because no strong empirical support for alternative hypothesis concerning cultural values can be made, they asserted that education may be seen as a tool to overcome restrictions in upward mobility in careers or jobs. In other words, the conformity these youth present may be more functional, as a human capital investment rather than the cultural meaning previously assumed. (2011)

UNDERREPRESENTATION OF ASIAN AMERICANS IN LAW PARTNER/EXECUTIVE FIRM POSITIONS

The previous researchers stressed the value of Asian culture including collectivism, strict family structure, respect to higher persons and emotional prohibition (Kim, Atkinson, & Yang, 1999; Sue & Sue, 2003). Asian traditional collectivistism and America's individual culture are contradictory and Asian Americans have greater challenges.

Unable to locate in a law firm or make career advancement poses a problem for professional graduates in view of the debt they have accumulated during their studies. In the 1980s and 1990s, law school tuitions increased significantly, but the number of law office jobs began to decline in 2004 before the recession. The demand for new lawyers has not been increasing even though the economy has gotten better (Caplan, 2012). Furthermore, the high tuition fees for law schools have resulted in heavy debts for law school students. After finishing their degrees, these high achievers find it hard to reclaim their training costs. It is hard for them in the current job market to locate even a stable position. According to Kay, Alarie, and Adjei (2013), lawyers who leave their career early face debts and no established career and career enhancement. It is doubtful if they can be paid back for their tuition investment.

This situation may lead young Asian professionals not to choose their desired career. In particular, the public service sector can be impacted by students' career choices because of the sector's low salaries compared to the private sector. Many law school graduates have more than $80,000 in law school loans when they graduate, but this is prevents graduates from entering public service jobs, which traditionally offer lower salaries (American Bar Association, 2003).

Heavy debts may seriously impact job dissatisfaction and employee retention. Job dissatisfaction would be a main reason for employee turnover and resignation (Bentein, Vandenberghe, Vandenberg, & Stinglhamber, 2005; Boswell, Boudreau, & Tichy, 2005; Griffeth, Hom, & Gaertner, 2000).

Coupled with the shift of the global labor market in the high-tech and manufacturing sectors, Asian Americans are more willing to take positions in their original countries. The increase of economic development in East Asia, especially in China and South Korea, has lured Asian Americans who cannot locate desired positions in their own countries. More often than not, these returns are not a one-way direction because their professional or family connections remain in the United States (Saxenian, 2005; Varrel,

2011). These highly-skilled Asian Americans have built a global and professional community based on their ethnic origin. It is the brain circulation induced by the glass ceiling.

SOLUTIONS AND RECOMMENDATIONS

In fact, Asian Americans show limited career and degree choices. Tang, Fouad, and Smith (1999) indicated that the three top careers of Asian Americans were engineer, physician, and computer scientist. Also, only a limited number of Asian Americans are social service workers (U.S. Census Bureau, 2007). Therefore, career development has been helpful in providing opportunities to develop their abilities, new skills, and new knowledge, and to find out their potential (Kular, Gatenby, Rees, Soane, & Truss, 2008).

As Asian Americans may not choose their career just based on their career interests (Leong & Serafica, 1995), there is a need for companies to have specialized talent development programs to meet the needs of Asian Americans' interests and to reflect their characteristics. This can be aligned with the goal of career development so as to enhance the knowledge and skills of Asian American employees. In particular, an early career after a first degree is critical for an individual's overall career (London, 1985). Also, early careers must be significant, as developmental experiences can have a long-term influence on career progress (Howard & Bray, 1988).

According to Pruis (2011), career development can be helpful for talent deployment at organizations and can meet the desires for professional development of the organizations' talent. For an example, Proctor & Gamble (P&G) has career support programs for Asian Americans including mentoring, conferences, and annual events. Diverse programs to enhance Asian Americans' career development and progression have been implemented (P&G, n.d.).

Talent development programs are related to organizational talent management and include career development, mentoring and coaching. Mentoring for talent to grow and excel in their development is one of the desired talent development programs. At the university level, there are mentoring programs for Asian Americans. At Pomona College, Asian American students can learn the leadership aspects of communication, planning, team building, and training together with Asian Americans' history, identity, and race (Liang, Lee, & Ting, 2002).

Through mentoring programs and experience, various aspects of business for Asian Americans can be improved. In particular, mentoring programs operated in the field of law can provide useful practices for Asian Americans' talent development. While individual law firms have general mentoring programs targeted for newly hired lawyers to achieve their extensive and diverse experiences from more experienced lawyers, there are also mentoring programs more specialized for Asian American lawyers on a local or regional basis. For example, the Asian American Bar Association in the San Francisco Bay area has mentoring programs for current law school students as well as young attorneys who have started their careers. Mentees who are law school students and young attorneys are paired with more senior attorneys for professional and personal development. The association offers events to promote the mentoring relationships, including brunches and karaoke. These activities can help build networks and find career paths (Asian American Bar, n.d.).

The American Bar Association's Office of Diversity and Inclusion holds their fall legal career development expo targeted at law students and young talents, which includes information for career development sessions and job search skills.

Asian Americans have and image as less assertive but passive people (Zane, Sue, Hu, & Kwon, 1991). These images could hamper them in taking leadership roles by making Asian Americans stay as team members rather than becoming leaders regardless of their high educational levels. Asian Americans are more likely to register for first-tier universities and to obtain higher degrees (Sakamoto, Goyette, & Kim, 2009). In particular, Asian American men have been disadvantaged from obtaining managerial positions and have taken lower supervising positions compared to White men (Takei & Sakamoto, 2009). For instance, the Chamber of Commerce has leadership development programs for Asian Americans are exemplary in addressing this issue. The Greater Dallas Asian American Chamber of Commerce has a Leadership Tomorrow program for Asian American future leaders in terms of network, leadership skills, and community involvement (Greater Dallas Asian American Chamber of Commerce, n.d.).

Sometimes, the important influence of family may work as a limiting factor for young people's career choices (Yee, Debaryshe, Yuen, Kim, & McCubbin, 2007). Asian Americans are more collectivistic and group oriented, which is contrary to White Americans who are more individual (Cartier, 2009). This collectivistic culture may hamper Asian Americans in certain roles such as leaders and managers, which require individual decisions and approaches, especially in corporate sectors (Henderson & Chan, 2005).

As the influence of peers and family is strong, how to confront family conflicts related to career decisions is critical. Career advising and awareness programs from high school and colleges for this population are desirable (Leong & Serafica, 1995). They need to have open communication with their family members about their career choices and to have the most updated career information.

CURRENT AND FUTURE TRENDS

Asian Americans sometimes regard the financial aspects in determining their young family members' careers choices that lead to job choices based on numerical values rather than career interest (Lee, 2013). Indeed, there are fewer available opportunities compared to Caucasians (Fouad & Bryars-Winston, 2005). Leong (1991) found that Asian American college students regard income and job status highly. Indeed, many Asian American students registered for postsecondary institutions in the United States and are hardworking people. There are fewer available opportunities compared to Caucasians (Fouad & Bryars-Winston, 2005), and a few people can take leadership positions. Asian American college graduates are more likely than White college graduates to be jobless (U.S. Department of Labor, 2011). Therefore, more career development programs must be focused on Asian Americans in their early educational stages. But only a limited number of researchers have studied for Asian American leadership development. Previous career development studies have targeted Japanese and Chinese, because their ethnic groups have longer histories in the United States. But we should be careful when generalizing the result of specific group targeted studies to the whole Asian Americans (Au, 2007).

It must be critical to help Asian Americans experience various aspects of business as they do not have full access to leadership positions. To address their lack of Asian American leaders, large companies like GE and AT&T have specific leadership development programs for them. GE has a program to provide professional development for Asian Americans using forum and initiative. Also, AT&T has special career advancement programs for Asians that offer more leadership opportunities and impact issues related to Asian Americans (AT&T, n.d.). The role of interdependence and peers for practical information can be meaningful especially for poor Asian American youth (Okubo, Yeh, Lin, Fujita, & Shea, 2007).

For a more successful talent development strategy, cooperation from diverse stakeholders will be useful. In particular, Asian professional organizations, such as Ascend, meet the changing needs of talent development for Asian Americans. Ascend has various initiatives, job fairs, mentoring programs, and leadership development programs to empower Asian Americans and promote their talent development. In the STEM field, there are diverse associations to promote networking and leadership: Asian American Architects and Engineers Association, Asian Pacific American Medical Students Association, Korean American Scientists and Engineers Association, and Silicon Valley Indian Professionals Association.

In particular, expanding services and information in relevant languages other than English has been conducted as some Asian Americans have indicated they lack English skills. One-stop career centers have provided multilingual services related to workforce program services. The U.S. Equal Employment Commission (2012) has also highlighted the importance of career development opportunities and training, and specific action plans for promotion, outreach, and recruitment for Asian Americans as follows:

- For federal careers, there are student educational employment programs and internships under the Pathways for Students and Recent Graduates for entry-level positions of Asian Americans.
- Executive development programs like the Federal Executive Leadership Program by the Office of Personnel Management and the Graduate School USA Leadership Development Programs have been recommended for best practices.

These practices can be applied to private companies as well to help overcome barriers that Asian Americans may face.

CONCLUSION

Talent development stresses development strategies to make sure the organization has enough talent supplies and development activities aligned with the talent management of the organization (Garavan, Carbery, & Rock, 2012). To address talent development issues for Asian Americans, there must be a consideration for the characteristics of Asian Americans, and more specialized talent development programs for Asian Americans are needed.

Empowering Asian Americans for their professional development must be the first priority to maximize their talents and enhance their careers. For their talent development, career development must be encouraged. It is important to help them navigate between their culture of origin and the main American culture (Fouad et al., 2008). Biculturalism in the Asian American career decision-making process will be necessary for career decisions (Okubo, Yeh, Lin, Fujita, & Shea, 2007). Sometimes, the high influence of family may work as a limiting factor in young people's career choices (Yee, DeBaryshe, Yuen, Kim, & McCubbin, 2007). As the influence of family values is strong, how to confront family conflicts related to career decisions can be a critical issue. They need to have open communication with their family members about their career choices and have the most updated career information.

Providing role models and mentors who can show various career paths can be helpful to promote talent development for young Asian Americans. In addition, networking opportunities will be valuable for finding more job opportunities for Asian Americans.

So far, only a limited number of studies have included Asian Americans' career development based on leadership development, and there is a need to pay more attention to young Asian Americans' career development in various fields. Also, there is an increasing need for career development studies related to Asian Americans in STEM because the Asian Americans' presence is growing (Au, 2007).

More career advising and the providing of role models can be helpful for diverse career choices and the development for Asian Americans who want to be lawyers. More systemized career development programs are necessary for early career juris doctorates and the academia of HRD needs to pay more attention to this issue.

In addition, diversifying career information regarding the potential career issues of young Asian Americans can help with career choices and decisions. But HRD literature seldom deals with career development for Asian Americans, while previous literature has focused on career development and Asian Americans addressing career counseling (e. g., Okubo, Yeh, Lin, Fujita, & Shea, 2007).

Future researchers need to pay more attention and consider Asian Americans culture values and norms in their career development, because topics addressing gender and race among Asian Americans regarding career development has been lacking (Lee, 2013). Asian American men and women may have different career experiences resulting in large differences in their career decisions (Fouad et al., 2008).

Also, more career theories for Asian Americans would be necessary to explain further about their career development issues as there are no specific career theories for this population (Leong & Serafica, 1995). In addition, contextual factors in the career choices of Asian Americans must be considered and further explored. Type of industry and detailed demographic information may provide more insights about this issue. More attention and interest in talent development for Asian Americans are needed.

NOTES

1. Around 30% of Asian Americans report some form of race-based barrier to advancement. See https://www.whitehouse.gov/administration/eop/aapi/data/critical-issues
2. We specifically look into Asian Americans whose origins are China, Korea, Taiwan, and India. Because there are too diverse characteristics about the category of Asian Pacific islanders, it is hard to address specific talent development issues that include all Asian-Pacific islanders.

REFERENCES

American Bar Association. (2003). *Lifting the burden: Law student debt as a barrier to public service: The final report of the ABA commission on loan repayment and forgiveness.* Retrieved from http://www.abanet.org/legalservices/downloads/lrap/lrapfinalreport.pdf

Asian American Bar Association of the Greater Bay Area. (n.d.). *AABA 2015-2016 mentorship program.* Retrieved from http://www.aaba-bay.com/

AT&T. (n.d). *Diversity management.* Retrieved from http://www.att.com/gen/corporate-citizenship?pid=17762

Au, F. (2007). *Personality and cultural influences on social cognitive career variables for Asians/Asian Americans.* Dissertation Abstracts International: Section B: The Sciences and Engineering, *68*(12-B). 1024–1199

Barak, S. (2012, December 21). *Asian Americans dominating tech?* EETimes. Retrieved from http://www.eetimes.com/author.asp?section_id=36&doc_id=1286886

Beede, D., Julian, T., Khan, B., Lehrman, R., McKittrick, G., Langdon, D., & Doms, M. (2011). *Education Supports Racial and Ethnic Equality in STEM* (ESA Issue Brief #05-11). U.S. Department of Commerce, Economics and Statistics Administration.

Bentein, K., Vandenberghe, C., Vandenberg, R., & Stinglhamber, F. (2005). The role of change in the relationship between commitment and turnover: A latent growth modeling approach. *Journal of Applied Psychology, 90*(3), 468–482.

Boswell, W. R., Boudreau, J. W., & Tichy, J. (2005). The relationship between employee job change and job satisfaction: The honeymoon-hangover effect. *Journal of Applied Psychology, 90*(5), 882–892.

Caplan, L. (2012, July 15). An existential crisis for law schools, *The New York Times.* Retrieved from http://www.nytimes.com/2012/07/15/opinion/sunday/an-existential-crisis-for-law-schools.html?_r=0

Cartier, C. (2009). *Asian American men's gender role conflict: An investigation of racism-related stress* (Unpublished master's thesis). University of Wisconsin, Madison, Wisconsin.

Chanen, J. S. (2006). Early exits. *American Bar Association Journal.* Retrieved from http://www.abajournal.com/magazine/article/early_exits/

Chua, A. (2011). *Battle hymn of the tiger mother.* London, England: Bloomsbury.

Fouad, N., & Byars-Winston, A. (2005). Cultural context of career choice: Meta-analysis of race/ethnicity differences. *The Career Development Quarterly, 53*(3), 223–233.

Fouad, N. A., Kantamneni, N., Smothers, M. K., Chen, Y. L., Fitzpatrick, M. E., & Terry, S. (2008). Asian American career development: A qualitative analysis. *Journal of Vocational Behavior, 72,* 43–59.

Garavan, T. N., Carbery, R., & Rock, A. (2012). Mapping talent development: Definition, scope and architecture. *European Journal of Training and Development, 36*(1), 5–24.

Gee, B., Peck, D., & Wong, J. (2015). Hidden in plain sight: Asian American leaders in Silicon Valley. The Ascend Foundation. Retrieved from https://c.ymcdn.com/sites/ascendleadership.site-ym.com/resource/resmgr/Research/HiddenInPlainSight_Paper_042.pdf

General Electric. (n.d.). *Asian pacific American forum*. Retrieved from http://www.ge.com/careers/culture/diversity/asian-pacific-american-forum-apaf

Greater Dallas Asian American Chamber of Commerce, (n.d.). *Leadership tomorrow*. Retrieved from http://www.gdaacc.com/index.php?src=gendocs&ref=LeadershipTomorrow&category=Involvement

Griffeth, R. W., Hom, P. W., & Gaertner, S. (2000). A meta-analysis of antecedents and correlates of employee turnover: Update, moderator tests, and research implications for the next millennium. *Journal of Management, 26*(3), 463–488.

Henderson, S. J., & Chan, A., (2005). Career happiness among Asian Americans: The interplay between individualism and interdependence. *Journal of Multicultural Counseling & Development, 33*(3), 180–192.

Howard, A., & Bray, D. W. (1988). *Managerial lives in transition: Advancing age and changing times: Adult development and aging*. New York, NY: Guilford Press.

Kay, F. M, Alarie, S., & Adjei, J. (2013). *Leaving law and barriers to re-entry: A study of departures from and re-entries to private practice. A report to the law society of upper Canada*, Retrieved from www.lsuc.on.ca/WorkArea/DownloadAsset.aspx?id=2147494539

Kim, H. K. (2013). *The experience of Korean American first born or only sons in the United States: Privilege or burden?* (Unpublished doctoral dissertation). State University of New York, Stony Brook.

Kim, B. S. K., Atkinson, D. R., & Yang, P. H. (1999). The Asian values scale: Development, factor analysis, validation, and reliability. *Journal of Counseling Psychology, 46*(3), 342–352.

Kular, S., Gatenby, M., Rees, C., Soane, E., & Truss, K. (2008). *Employee engagement: A literature review*. Working Paper Series No. 19. London, England: Kingston University. Retrieved from http://eprints.kingston.ac.uk/4192/1/19wempen.pdf

Lee, S. Y (2013). *The career development of Asian American female visual artists*. Unpublished doctoral dissertation, The University of Iowa, Iowa City, IA.

Leong, F. T. (1991) Career development attributes and occupational values of Asian American and White American college students. *Career Development Quarterly, 39*(3), 221–230.

Leong, F. T., & Serafica, F. C. (1995) Career development of Asian Americans: A research area in need of a good theory. In F. T. Leong (Ed.), *Career development and vocational behavior of ethnic minorities*. Mahwah, NJ: Lawrence Erlbaum.

Leung, S. A., Ivey, D., & Suzuki, L. (1994). Factors affecting the career aspirations of Asian Americans. *Journal of Counseling & Development, 72*(4), 404–410.

Liang, C. T. H., Lee, S., & Ting, M. P. (2002). Developing Asian American leaders. *New Directions for Student Services, 2002*(97), 81–90

London, M. (1985). *Developing managers: A guide to motivating and preparing people for successful managerial careers*. San Francisco, CA: Jossey-Bass.

Loo, A. M. (2005). *The role of culture and gender in the career choice of Asian American women* (Unpublished doctoral dissertation). The Wright Institute, Berkeley, CA

Lynham, S. A., & Cunningham, P. W. (2006). National human resource development in transitioning societies in the developing world: Concept and challenges. *Advances in Developing Human Resources, 8*(1), 116–135.

McLean, G. N. (2004). National human resource development: What in the world is it? *Advances in Developing Human Resources, 6*(3), 269–275.

National Science Foundation. (2013). *Scientists and engineers statistical data system.* Retrieved from https://www.nsf.gov/statistics/sestat/

Okubo, Y., Yeh, C. J., Lin, P.-Y., & Fujita, K. (2007). The career decision-making process of Chinese American youth. *Journal of Counseling & Development, 85*(4), 440–449.

Proctor & Gamble. (n.d.). *U.S. info diversity, Asian or Pacific Americans,* Retrieved from http://pg.sitebase.net/us/diversity/asian/pages/content/resources.html

Prius, E. (2011). The five key principles for talent development. *Industrial and Commercial Training, 43*(4), 206–216.

Sakamoto, A., Goyette, K. A., & Kim C. (2009). The socioeconomic attainments of Asian Americans. *Annual Review of Sociology, 35,* 255–276.

Saxenian, A. (2005). From brain drain to brain circulation: Transnational communities and regional upgrading in India and China. *Studies in Comparative International Development, 40*(2), 35–61.

Sue, D. W., & Sue, D. (2003). *Counseling the culturally different: Theory and practice.* New York, NY: Wiley.

Sue, S., & Okazaki, S. (1990). Asian-American educational achievements: A phenomenon in search of an explanation. *American Psychologist, 45*(8), 913–920.

Takei, I., & Sakamoto A. (2009, May). *Demographic characteristics of third-generation Asian Americans: Socioeconomic attainments and assimilation.* Paper presented at the 2009 Population Association of America annual meeting, Detroit, MI.

Tang, M., Fouad, N. A., & Smith, P. L. (1999). Asian Americans' career choices: A path model to examine factors influencing their career choices. *Journal of Vocational Behavior, 54*(1), 142–157.

U.S. Census Bureau. (2011). *American community survey,* Retrieved from http://www.acs.census.gov/acs

U.S. Census Bureau. (2007). *Statistical abstract of the United States: 2007.* Retrieved from http://www.census.gov/library/publications/2006/compendia/statab/126ed.html

U.S. Department of Labor. (2011). *The Asian American labor force in the recovery.* U.S. Department of Labor. Retrieved from https://www.dol.gov/_sec/media/reports/AsianLaborForce/AsianLaborForce.pdf

U.S. Equal Employment Opportunity Commission. (2012). *A practical guide to addressing common issues and possible barriers which Asian and native Hawaiian or other Pacific Islander employees may face in the federal work force.* Retrieved from http://www.eeoc.gov/federal/reports/aapi_practical_guide.cfm

Varrel, A. (2011). Gender and intergenerational issues in the circulation of highly skilled migrants: the case of Indian IT professionals. In *Gender, Generations and the Family in International Migration* (pp. 335–353). Amsterdam, the Netherlands: Amsterdam University Press.

Yee, B. W. K., DeBaryshe, B. D., Yuen, S., Kim, S., & McCubbin, H. (2007). American and Pacific Islander families. In F. Leong, A. G. Inman, A. Ebreo, L. Yang, L. M. Kinoshita, & M. Fu (Eds.), *Handbook of Asian American psychology* (2nd ed., pp. 69–86). Thousand Oaks, CA: Sage.

Zane, N., Sue, S., Hu, L., & Kwon, J. (1991). Asian American assertion: A social learning analysis of cultural differences. *Journal of Counseling Psychology, 38*, 63–70.

CHAPTER 6

MAXIMIZING MOTIVATION

Talent Development in Nongovernmental Organizations

Jill Zarestky and Shannon Deer

Nongovernmental organizations (NGOs) operate along a spectrum, from local, grassroots efforts to billion-dollar international organizations, but as a whole are responsible for much of the service and social justice work in developing or underserved regions. Many exist to fill a gap in services left by government and for-profit organizations. As service providers with income streams dependent on charitable donations or grant funding, many NGOs and their employees operate without the resources of comparably sized for-profit organizations (Anheier & Salamon, 2006; Lewis, 2003; Schepers et al., 2005).

The purpose of this chapter is to explore NGO talent development strategies with an emphasis on the specific circumstances and challenges faced by NGOs. While strategies of talent development have been previously applied to human resource development (HRD) and business contexts, what remains is an analysis of those strategies for the specific needs and constraints of NGOs. We have drawn from existing conceptions of talent development and motivational theory to envision how those conceptions

Talent Development and the Global Economy:
Perspectives from Special Interest Groups, pp. 75–92
Copyright © 2017 by Information Age Publishing
All rights of reproduction in any form reserved.

should evolve to support NGOs' needs. We hope our recommendations will add to NGO management and HRD philosophies and encourage future research from a perspective uniquely different from existing management and HRD practices.

In the following sections, we begin with a description of the circumstances and characteristics that differentiate NGOs from for-profit organizations and other nonprofits, with an emphasis on the aspects of NGO operations that pertain to talent development. Specifically, we explore NGO structures, management and HRD practices, and employee motivation. We then provide a brief overview of talent development as it relates to employee motivation. Finally, we provide recommendations for talent development strategies that meet the specific needs of NGOs.

WHAT IS A NONGOVERNMENTAL ORGANIZATION?

Defining an NGO is a complex and highly debated task. As a consequence, NGOs are more often defined by what they are not—governmental or for profit—than what they are (Vakil, 1997). NGOs are typically considered a subset of the nonprofit sector, also called the third sector (Anheier & Salamon, 2006). The nonprofit sector includes both NGOs and other nonprofit organizations (NPOs), but distinguishing between NGOs and other NPOs has presented challenges to scholars. While in general, some convergence between the term NGO and NPO has occurred (Najam, 2000), the terms are frequently, but inappropriately, used as synonyms (Salamon & Anheier, 1997; Vakil, 1997).

The most widely adopted NPO definition was developed by Salamon and Anheier (1997) who identified five key characteristics of NPOs: formally organized, independent from the government, nonprofit distributing, self-governing, and reliant on voluntary involvement. The degree to which organizations adhere to these five characteristics will vary. Vakil (1997) argued NGOs may not fit into three of the five NPO characteristics identified by Salamon and Anheier (1997). First, some NGOs are informal, community organizations. Vakil (1997) specifically referenced burial societies and savings clubs as examples of such informal organizations often considered NGOs. Second, cooperatives are commonly considered NGOs. Although, profit generation is not the primary goal of cooperatives or other NGOs, cooperatives do distribute profits to their members. Finally, not all NGOs rely on volunteers, as the NGO sector has become increasingly professionalized.

Based on Vakil's (1997) exclusion of the nonprofit-distributing, formal, and voluntary criteria for NGOs compared to other NPOs, one may conclude NGOs are more inclusive than NPOs. However, there is another critical distinction to consider. NGOs have historically been viewed as organizations "engaged in the promotion of economic and social development" (Salamon & Anheier, 1997, p. 129). According to Vakil, the development focus of the NGO sector excludes unions or professional groups and any strictly cultural, recreational, or religious NPOs without development missions. Further NGO definitions have historically only included organizations operating in the developing world (Salamon & Anheier, 1997). More recently, geographic distinctions have become less relevant with recognition of organizations in developed countries as NGOs as well.

For purposes of this chapter, we adapted Vakil's (1997) working definition and consider NGOs as self-governing organizations, to some degree separate from government, with their primary missions focused on some facet of development and empowerment of people, rather than profit generation. We do consider NGOs to be a distinct subsector of NPOs and the nonprofit sector. Therefore, in addition to utilizing studies specifically about NGOs, we also utilize scholarship referencing the nonprofit sector in general and provide customized applications for NGOs. We recognize there are many nuances and differences across the community of NGOs, and do not presume to believe our recommendations will be uniformly successful or appropriate for all NGOs. Additionally, we characterize differences between NGOs and for-profit organizations, which are critical to consider when adapting HRD principles designed for the for-profit sector to NGOs.

DIFFERENCES BETWEEN NGOs AND FOR-PROFIT ORGANIZATIONS

Management Services for Health (1998, p. 2) defined HRD in NGOs as the need to "recruit, maintain and develop employees in order for the organization to meet its desired goals," which is a statement that holds true for most any multinational for-profit corporation. However, NGOs fundamentally differ from for-profit organizations in many ways. Understanding how the two sectors differ is important when considering HRD interventions for NGOs. In particular, as Lewis (2003) asserted, if NGOs uncritically adopt management techniques from business, they run the risk of compromising "NGOs' abilities to provide critical voice and promote good development" (p. 342). Although certainly NGOs share some characteristics of for-profit organizations and they pursue development goals, such as globalized operations and employees from a variety of cultures and nations, the emphasis here draws primarily from the differing business context of work. In the following sections, we will present the structural and operational differences, differences in management and HRD practices, and differences in employee motivation.

Structure and Operations

There are many structural and operational differences between NGOs and for-profit organizations. These differences are highlighted in three of the five characteristics of NPOs identified by Salamon and Anheier (1997) and adapted by Vakil (1997): (a) unlike for-profit organizations NGOs primary focus is not profit generation or distribution, (b) NGOs are not controlled by shareholders as are many for-profit organizations, and (c) NGOs often rely on volunteers whereas all employees are paid in for-profit organizations. Perhaps, the primary difference between NGOs and for-profit organizations is their raison d'être (De Cooman, De Geiter, Pepermans, & Jegers, 2011). For-profit organizations exist to create financial earnings to distribute to shareholders. In contrast, NGOs are not motivated by profit, but by very specific social or development missions.

As a consequence of not focusing on profits, NGOs are typically more resource constrained than their for-profit counterparts (Anheier & Salamon, 2006; Lewis, 2003; Schepers et al., 2005). Since most NGOs reinvest all income back into the organization, focus on a social mission, and negotiate limited resources, NGOs' ability to pay employees is often more limited than in for-profit organizations. The first financial priority for NGOs is reinvesting funds received or generated back into the organization's constituents to accomplish the organization's goals. Therefore, NGO employees rarely receive bonuses or other incentive pay. Opportunities for promotion are more limited for nonprofit employees than for personnel working in for-profit organizations (De Cooman et al., 2011), and NPOs are more likely to make promotion decisions based on seniority rather than on performance, as is the practice in many for-profit organizations (Devaro & Brookshire, 2007). Additionally, lateral movements may be less available, limiting NGO employees' opportunities for professional growth through cross-training (De Cooman et al., 2011). Before we make recommendations for how NGOs can alternatively incentivize talent development, we first address additional key differences between the sectors in the following two sections: management and HRD practices, and employee personality and behavioral differences.

Management and HRD Practices

In addition to the contested definition of NGOs, NGO management is also a highly debated topic. Scholars investigating NGO management have long drawn from the principles of business management, also referred to as generic management, used by for-profit organizations (Lewis, 2003). According to Lewis (2003), NGOs "face distinctive challenges of structure and context which means that generic management ideas may not always apply" (p. 340). Three additional relevant management philosophies exist: (a) third sector management, targeting NPOs; (b) public management specific to government operations; and (c) development management for efforts designed or intended to reduce poverty. Alone, none of the four management techniques appear to satisfactorily increase efficiency and effectiveness in NGO management (Lewis, 2003). As a result, Lewis (2003) proposed development of a fifth discipline of management specific to NGOs. As NGOs have grown in frequency, size, and influence (Ronalds, 2010; Vakil, 1997), it is increasingly important to understanding NGOs as a distinct subsector (Lewis, 2003).

Given the fundamental differences between NGOs and for-profit business, we do not recommend NGOs apply generic management techniques and principles without critical consideration. However, we believe human resource development (HRD) can still provide relevant insight to NGO operations. We recommend NGOs consider existing HRD and talent development strategies when they face challenges common to all organizations, and critically adapt existing principles to appropriately fit their NGO when the context varies from for-profit. More focus should be given, in research and practice, to the adaptation of existing HRD principles to meet NGO needs (Lewis, 2003). We seek to support such work by recommending appropriate adaptations later in this chapter.

EMPLOYEE MOTIVATION

Numerous scholars have claimed nonprofit employees are more intrinsically motivated than for-profit employees (Leete, 2000; Mirvis & Hackett, 1983; Valentinov, 2007). Previous findings suggested NPOs disproportionately rely on employees who are more oriented toward intrinsic motivation than extrinsic motivation (Leete, 2000). However, more recently researchers have questioned these findings based on a limited, dichotomous exploration of only intrinsic and extrinsic motivation (e.g., Devaro & Brookshire, 2007; De Cooman et al., 2011). In the following sections, we will present the different types of motivation, and then discuss the applications of research about motivation to employees in NGOs and for-profit organizations.

Types of Motivation

Intrinsic motivation is motivation from within an employee without any obvious link to external rewards, often based on personal interest or enjoyment. Extrinsic motivation results in an employee acting based on anticipated external rewards or incentives, which could be monetary (e.g., bonuses or promotions) or social (e.g., praise or status). Ryan and Deci (2000) identified additional motivation types as they relate to the authors' self-determination theory, described as "the investigation of people's inherent growth tendencies ... that are the basis for their self-motivation" (p. 68). Intrinsic motivation and extrinsic motivation are included in their theory along with four additional subdivisions of extrinsic motivation. These subdivisions vary in the degree to which the motivation is more external or internal and include (a) external regulation, (b) introjected regulation, (c) identified regulation, and (d) integrated regulation.

Ryan and Deci (2000) described self-regulation as how people incorporate social values and external influences into their own value systems and motivations. External regulation is consistent with traditional definitions of extrinsic motivation in individuals motivated by external rewards and punishment. Introjected regulation involves "taking in a regulation but not fully accepting it as one's own" (p. 72). Behaviors relate to maintaining self-esteem and are driven by an effort to avoid guilt and anxiety or to boost one's ego. Identified regulation reflects a personal, conscious adoption of a goal or regulation as one's own. Finally, integrated regulation, which Ryan and Deci designated as most critical, "occurs when identified regulations are fully assimilated to the self, which means they have been evaluated and brought into congruence with one's other values and needs" (p. 73). Integrated regulation is similar to traditionally defined intrinsic motivation. However, the scholars have classified integrated motivation as external because the actor is seeking valued outcomes separate from the defining characteristic of intrinsic motivation: engaging in an activity for personal enjoyment.

Applying Motivation

Based on new empirical evidence, understanding the distinctions between Ryan and Deci's (2000) types of external motivation is critical to understanding and applying to practice the differences in employee motivation in nonprofit and for-profit organizations. As previously mentioned, De Cooman et al. (2011) provided additional and contradictory insight into the commonly held belief that nonprofit employees had higher levels of intrinsic motivation than for-profit employees. Results from their study of 630 knowledge workers across many different industries and organizations showed employee's intrinsic motivation, as defined by Ryan and Deci (2000), did not vary across the nonprofit and for-profit sectors. However, De Cooman et al. (2011) did find nonprofit employees demonstrated more integrated and identified regulation and less external regulation than for-profit employees. Consistent with the findings showing greater integrated and identified regulation, De Cooman et al. found nonprofit employees were more concerned with altruism and demonstrated a better person-organization fit than employees working in for-profit organizations. In contrast to for-profit employees, nonprofit employees placed less emphasis on career advancement.

Schepers et al. (2005) supported many of De Cooman et al.'s (2011) findings, specifically those related to career advancement and motivation. Although Schepers et al. did not specifically use the terms integrated and identified regulation, they found nonprofit employees were more committed to their organization's philosophies and more motivated by the public good, corresponding to integrated or identified regulation, than were for-profit employees. Schepers et al. also found nonprofit employees were more people-oriented, more likely to help, and more forgiving than for-profit employees.

The differences between NGOs and the for-profit sector presented in this section form the foundation of our recommendations for talent development in NGOs later in this chapter. In particular, we wish to emphasize the need to design organizational practices using the motivation types presented by Ryan and Deci (2000) and supported by De Cooman et al. (2011), and away from the assumption that intrinsic motivation is higher with nonprofit workers than for-profit workers. Before we make recommendations, we introduce some key issues in talent development relevant to motivation.

TALENT DEVELOPMENT AND EMPLOYEE MOTIVATION

The literature on talent development is wide-ranging, indicative of a new area for research and practice that has yet to become well-defined (Nilsson & Ellström, 2012). Pruis (2011) suggested strong talent development programs are the result of consistent organizational talent management strategies and include, for example, resource planning, recruitment, career planning and development, and engagement, as well as learning and development.

Garavan, Carbery, and Rock (2012) presented a broad overview of talent development, as differentiated from but encompassing of talent management, and attempted to define its scope and key issues. The authors focused primarily on for-profit corporations and ultimately suggested five key dimensions for talent development in organizations, including (a) identifying individuals for participation and selection strategies, (b) choosing the competencies on which to focus, (c) defining whose needs take precedence and where responsibility lies, (d) establishing a time frame, and (e) designing a framework, structure, and sequence for the talent development process. While all five dimensions arguably are influential in the success of a comprehensive talent development initiative, we view the first dimension as critical to the process. HRD professionals should have an answer to the question "Who?" before designing development and management strategies to address the remaining four dimensions.

Talent development in corporations is most frequently used as a tool to identify and develop the next generation of executives or organizational leaders. As such, resources are often diverted toward key high-performing individuals rather than inclusive practices that seek to build the skills and contributions of all employees to the organization. Pruis (2011) advised that an approach focused on a few individuals is effective in the short term, particularly if there is an executive vacancy, but that in the long term, a broad, inclusive approach is more likely to be effective.

Pruis (2011) went so far as to generate a new definition for talent: "something intrinsic, something that reinforces itself and does not require appreciation from others" (p. 208). If we compare this definition to our prior discussion of employee motivation, Pruis's definition of talent is almost identical to definitions of intrinsic motivation and closely related to descriptions integrated and identified regulation (Ryan & Deci, 2000), and is then relevant to our discussion of the differences in this regard between NGO and for-profit employees. As such, it appears likely that a talent development strategy focused on employees with high intrinsic motivation, or integrated or identified regulation, would naturally also encompass talented employees.

Thus, a strong talent development program operating from the intersection of employee talent and motivation would seek to maximize and build from those employee qualities. Through HRD practices, organizations can create opportunities for challenging, meaningful assignments and establish supportive work environments for talent, the goal of which would be to improve employee capacities and foster commitment to jobs and the organization (Hiltrop, 1999). This synergy of talent and motivation is an excellent framework for the specific needs and context of NGO talent development.

RECOMMENDATIONS FOR NGO TALENT DEVELOPMENT

There is a paucity of research related to talent development in NGOs. Kim and McLean (2012) explicitly recommended HRD researchers explore talent-related practices in NPOs. They reasoned, most related research to date has focused on for-profit corporations rather than other types of organizations, such as NGOs. As previously argued, we believe NGO management issues need to be explored independent of generic business management given the general differences between NGOs and for-profit organizations. Therefore, we agree with Kim and McLean's call for specific research related to talent development in NGOs.

Before HRD scholars and practitioners can adapt for-profit sector talent development theories to NGO contexts, it is critical that HRD, as a field, explore the differences between the two sectors as they relate specifically to talent development issues. Based on the previous discussion of the ways in which NGOs, their employees, and their organizational needs differ from for-profit businesses, we have established the need for NGO-specific talent development practices. In this section, we make recommendations for what we believe NGO talent development priorities and strategies should be. Rather than taking a comprehensive approach, we emphasize the facets of talent development in NGOs that are most likely to differ from the general approaches of for-profit organizations, specifically talent management and employee motivation.

Targeted Talent Management

Talent management is a component of talent development. Garavan et al. (2012) emphasized the importance of incorporating talent management when considering an organization's talent development system. Recruitment and planning are context-sensitive talent management issues relevant to talent development.

Recruiting for Organizational Fit

A specific concern for NGO talent management is recruiting employees with motivation dispositions, such as integrated or identified regulation, aligned with an organization's mission. High integrated and identified regulation signifies an individual's internal commitment to an organization's mission and may indicate organizational fit. NGOs likely already recruit for person-organization fit, which has been identified as a common practice in NPOs (Devaro & Brookshire, 2007; Schepers et al., 2005). However, those organizations not already intentionally recruiting for organizational fit and high integrated or identified regulation may benefit from implementing thoughtful recruitment practices to identify such employee characteristics.

According to Mann (2006), identifying employees with high public service motivation (PSM) is a key component of talent management in NPOs. PSM includes an individual's "desire to make a difference," and motivation is based on organization's service mission, as well as other internal rather than external motivating factors (Mann, 2006, p. 33). However, PSM can be challenging to identify and cultivate; management may not be able to increase PSM in employees through incentives. Studies have shown that intrinsic interest in a task is often lowered when extrinsic rewards are linked to the activity (Pink, 2009) and subsequently, efforts to increase PSM are likely to have the opposite of the desired effect. Accordingly, some of the research predicated on the hypothesis that PSM is positively related to performance levels also predicts that extrinsic reward systems should have a negative effect on individuals with high PSM (Mann, 2006). Therefore, NGOs may benefit from recruiting individuals who already have a high propensity for PSM, rather than trying to incentivize or cultivate PSM.

McCulloch and Turban (2007) recommended assessing person-organization fit during the hiring process. Further, De Cooman et al. (2011) suggested offering prospective NPO employees a realistic organization preview, in addition to a preview of the job, so prospects can self-assess their fit with the organization. Kucherov and Zavyalova (2012) found that in for-profit companies with strong employer brands, brand served as a useful recruiting tool and a means of attracting talent. The philanthropic work of NGOs might serve a similar purpose in connecting the organization with like-minded potential employees. Similarly, Collings and Mellahi (2009) advocated for the importance of employee commitment and motivation as critical links between a talent management strategy and organization-level results. Such assessment tools and organization previews could improve retention as well as recruitment by providing prospective employees and employers with a basis for determining person-organization fit.

Planning

Planning is a critical component of talent management and includes succession planning, dependent on identifying future talent needs, as well as providing employees with skills development opportunities, and giving substantive feedback through performance reviews to which employees can respond or use as criteria for professional growth. According to Garavan et al. (2012), talent management involves a 5- to 7-year planning process. NGOs may find it particularly difficult to plan so far in advance given the challenging environments in which they typically operate. Given that donors periodically reevaluate and shift funding strategies (AbouAssi, 2012), NGO operations are highly sensitive to changing beneficiary needs and sources of available funding (Koch, Dreher, Nunnenkamp, & Thiele, 2009). Shifts in funding or beneficiary circumstances may create significant disparity between an NGO's anticipated and actual talent needs. Recruiting for flexibility and adaptability may be necessary in addition to recruiting for employees motivated by the organization's mission. In the following section, we will provide additional recommendations for utilizing employee's natural motivation tendencies to benefit the NGO and its constituents.

MAXIMIZING THE ADVANTAGES OF EMPLOYEE MOTIVATION

Related to talent development specifically, we propose NGOs could benefit tremendously from fostering employee motivation with the proper incentives. Although financial security through work is equally attractive to for-profit and nonprofit workers, achieving financial prosperity is a more salient motivation factor for for-profit employees (De Cooman et al., 2011). Therefore, bonuses and raises may effectively motivate for-profit employees, but likely not NGO employees. We encourage NGOs to consider alternative strategies for cultivating employee motivation by focusing not on financial incentives but on person-organization fit, as previously described, and job satisfaction from meaningful work.

The discussion in this section focuses on recommendations that enable organizations to recruit and harness employees' motivation in NGOs. While understanding employee motivation is an important component of talent development for organizations in all sectors, employee motivation is the most closely related research stream to talent development in NGOs. We have previously discussed extant research highlighting the differences between motivation factors in NGOs and for-profit organizations. Next, we will make recommendations for practice that is developed from the literature.

Ryan and Deci (2000) argued employees with motivation classified as integrated or identified regulation seek autonomy, competence, and relatedness in order to consider their work meaningful and to maintain motivation; Pink (2009) labeled the same concepts as autonomy, mastery, and purpose. NGOs are well positioned to deliver these three qualities of meaningful work. Giancola (2011) connects Pink (2009) and Ryan and Deci's (2000) qualities of motivating work to the top drivers of employee engagement. Giancola (2011) found that of the top 10 drivers, all of them correlate to Ryan and Deci's qualities of meaningful work. If an NGO talent development program recruits employees with strong organizational fit and high integrated or identified regulation, the organization should be well positioned to provide the employee with engaging and satisfying work. To keep employees in for-profit organizations engaged and satisfied though, a well-defined career path, including promotion, is significant. The importance and implementation of promotions may be quite different in NGOs.

Promotions

Promotions in the for-profit sector tend to be based on performance, but in the nonprofit sector, promotions tend to be based on seniority (De Cooman et al., 2011; Devaro & Brookshire, 2007). Additionally, fewer promotions occur in nonprofit settings compared to for-profit settings. Possible reasons for fewer promotions include NGOs limited resources for pay increases and a less hierarchical organizational structure. Performance-based promotions may be particularly challenging for NGOs, because work performance is a challenging construct to measure (Chen, 2012) and is based on reviewer subjectivity (Garavan et al., 2012). Therefore, the NGO environment may be less appealing to employees motivated by growth, resulting in nonprofit employees who are less growth oriented (De Cooman et al., 2011).

Based on what we know about the nonprofit sector compared to the for-profit sector, on average NGO employees are likely to have fewer opportunities for promotions, may recognize promotions are frequently based on seniority rather than performance (Devaro & Brookshire, 2007), and work in an environment relatively "less favorable for individuals with high growth needs" (De Cooman et al., 2011, p. 229). Additionally, NGO employees are less motivated by external factors such as promotions and incentives (De Cooman et al., 2011) and their pre-existing motivation may even be undermined by such policies (Pink, 2009). Based on these differences, we recommend NGOs explore other criteria besides solely focusing on performance, which is hard to measure, and seniority to determine candidates for promotion.

One option would be for NGOs to consider integrated and identified regulation as a promotion criteria as it relates to commitment to the organization's mission. Under such a model, the more committed an individual is to the organization's mission, the more in line the mission becomes with his or her own values, and the more likely he or she would be earn a promotion. A promotion structure based on commitment to the mission could encourage person-organizational fit and harness the motivation already most salient for nonprofit employees. A word of caution here is organizational leaders need to be careful using external motivators, such as promotions, to encourage individuals with integrated or identified regulation. Ryan and Deci (2000) classified these incentives as extrinsic motivation rewards, but in some cases external incentives have been found to reduce task-related intrinsic motivation (Pink, 2009). Organizations should be careful in the way they implement external rewards for the forms of motivation that are more intrinsically oriented.

Another option could be implementing job redesign, which has also been an effective motivational tool across all three sectors: nonprofit, for-profit, and governmental (Perry, Mesch, & Paarlberg, 2006). NGOs could utilize job redesign even without incorporating upward mobility. Lateral movement or integration of new job responsibilities could allow an NGO employee additional cross-training opportunities within the organization. These development opportunities may be more comfortable or feasible for individuals without high growth needs and organizations with less hierarchical structures. Similarly, employee independence and autonomy may be a useful trade-off for NGOs that cannot offer a well-defined career ladder.

Autonomy

As one of the three qualities of work Ryan and Deci (2000) and Pink (2009) recommended for engaged and motivated employees, autonomy is an advantage in NGO operations. As NGOs are typically more resource constrained than their for-profit counterparts (Anheier & Salamon, 2006; Lewis, 2003; Schepers et al., 2005), employees may need to demonstrate independence and self-reliance in negotiating around those constrained resources. Since NGO employees are often asked to demonstrate autonomy in their work, it is reasonable to expect that they could also demonstrate autonomy in their development.

Garavan et al. (2012) advocated a need for employees to "shift from organizationally managed to self-managed development" (p. 15). This autonomy may manifest in terms of an individual's "self-awareness, self-confidence and persistence" (p. 15) to identify and seek out learning and development opportunities. NGOs are more likely than for-profit companies to not only permit or encourage such development autonomy, but to depend on it. As NGO employees are encouraged to become more autonomous, it is also likely that they would be more interested and comfortable contributing their expertise and opinions to organizational decision-making processes.

Participation in Decision Making

Perry et al. (2006) found increasing participation, defined as greater employee involvement in decision-making, had a significant impact on affective aspects of motivation, a moderate impact on job performance, and a significant impact on decision-making ability. Participation enhances exposure, which Garavan et al. (2012) found to be an effective talent development mechanism. Garavan et al. described exposure as an opportunity "to experience different organizational, cultural, cross-cultural, and work practice situations" by working in "different contexts and situations"

(p. 11). Perry et al. enhanced exposure by encouraging the different contexts and situations required for involvement in high-level organizational decision-making. Participation could be used by NGOs as a talent development strategy to prepare employees for higher level management. Participation can also allow NGOs to further harness and enhance employees' integrated and identified regulation by allowing them to see how difficult decisions relate to the organization's mission to which the employees are committed. Perry et al. (2006) also found participation gave a greater voice to lower-level employees, which in addition to improving talent development could enhance the democratic values and practices many NGOs strive to achieve.

Challenges

Pruis (2011) recommended successful talent development programs not only incorporate an awareness of potential challenges, but also consciously build upon them as a demonstration of managerial foresight. In the following sections, we highlight some open issues for NGO talent development requiring additional consideration and investigation in future research and practice.

Limited Resources

Compared to for-profit organizations, NGOs typically operate in resource scarce environments or with fewer resources in general (Anheier & Salamon, 2006; Lewis, 2003; Schepers et al., 2005). Challenges for NGOs attempting to implement talent development practices include an inability to offer wages competitive with for-profit organizations and insufficient resources for initiatives that are not critical to the NGO's social mission. Similarly, geographic areas where NGOs are needed are often less developed or conflict ridden. Potential local employees may lack formal education or professional experience, and therefore, in addition to limited financial resources, human resources may also be limited. Additional challenges specific to NGOs talent development efforts stem from their organizational structure.

Nonhierarchical Structures

NGOs tend to be structurally flatter than their more hierarchical for-profit counterparts (Devaro & Brookshire, 2007). Garavan et al. (2012) referred to the talent development pipeline when expressing the need for planning related to promotions and succession planning. The pipeline concept may not work for NGOs with flat structures, because there may not be a hierarchy in place for a clear promotion path. As a result, NGOs may consider advancing employees' experiences over advancing positions. As stated in the previous section, broadening employees experiences through participation (Perry et al., 2006) or the similar concept of exposure (Garavan et al., 2012) may also be a better complement to NGO employees' motivation than promotion through titles or positions. However, exposing NGO employees to varying experiences is not without its challenges.

Exposure

The amount of exposure NGO employees can obtain will depend on the organization. In this context, exposure means simply "the opportunities to work in different contexts and situations" (Garavan et al., 2012, p. 11). NGOs operating in multiple regions, using multiple approaches to benefit constituents, and thus facing a greater variety of challenges, will have the greater opportunity for employee exposure. Lateral and cross-training opportunities may be more limited in less complex or more highly specialized NGOs. However, all NGOs are likely to be faced with challenging decisions. Involving employees in decision-making as previously recommended, even if involvement does not involve changes in the employees' location, department, or supervisor, will increase their exposure.

Increasing exposure may not seem like the most efficient talent development tool. Learning new tasks, or getting used to a new department or region, requires time, whereas fostering focused employee expertise is more efficient in the short run. NGOs with limited financial and human resources may choose not to cross-train or rotate employees, but we assert increasing exposure is a worthwhile talent development investment. Garavan et al. (2012) argued involving NGO employees in developmental challenges and organizational hardships is important because such exposure increased employees' decision-making ability. Perry et al. (2006) showed participation to be highly effective in influencing effective change and moderately effective at improving performance. These findings suggest participation and exposure, while challenging, could lead to important improvements in employee talents and preparation for additional responsibilities. These potential improvements connect to the challenge of measuring performance for employees in the nonprofit sector.

Performance Measurement

Chen (2012) identified measuring performance as a challenge to influencing NPO employees' work attitudes. For-profit organizations often have explicitly clear goals, which primarily include increasing shareholder wealth. In contrast, NGOs goals often are complex and stakeholders, including individual donors, bilateral donors, multilateral donors, international governments, local governments, and beneficiaries may have conflicting interests. Conflicting interests and shifts in goals and funding strategies can make setting performance goals, let alone creating measurement tools, extremely challenging for NGOs. Challenges in measuring performance then make rewarding performance difficult (Chen, 2012), which may shape the types of employees interested in NGO work. As previously mentioned, NGO workers are less motivated by external incentives (such as promotions) and may be less growth oriented. Expanding NGOs' ability to measure performance could improve their ability to recruit individuals who are not only motivated by the organizations' mission, but also have the potential to become leaders in the organization.

CONCLUSION

There is a clear need for further research specific to NGO management and HRD (Kim & McLean, 2012; Lewis, 2003), including employee motivation, which has been our framework for considering NGO talent development. Further motivation research in HRD should explore the subcategories of intrinsic and extrinsic motivation identified by Ryan and Deci (2000), because the distinction between intrinsic motivation and integrated or identified regulation could be critical for NGOs (and other types of organizations) in implementing talent development strategies.

Of course, it is insufficient to evaluate only motivation and expect to provide NGOs with complete guidance for talent development. Given NGOs' unique talent development struggles such as recruitment, retention, nonhierarchical structures, and limited resources, future research should focus specifically on which practices are most effective in NGO talent development. NGO specific research could lead to great improvements for NGOs. With improved and researched strategies, NGOs could free time and energy to focus on their primary mission and still work toward improving talent development to benefit the organization and employees. Specifically, greater efficiency and improved employee performance could result from the recommendations we have provided by improving person-organization fit through recruiting for the motivation types most important for each NGO. Research and practice will benefit from NGOs being more transparent about their talent development and consciously considering the practices they currently have in place.

As NGOs become increasingly important to meeting the needs of populations in underserved areas and addressing the gap in services between government and for-profit industry, the skill levels and retention rates of high performing NGO employees will be paramount to sustainable, successful efforts. A strong model of talent development in NGOs is crucial to the long-term viability of many NGOs efforts. As we have presented, based upon the differences between NGOs and NPOs, NGOs and for-profit business, and the need for focused business management, clearly talent development cannot be one-size-fits-all.

REFERENCES

AbouAssi, K. (2012). Hands in the pockets of mercurial donors: NGOs response to shifting funding priorities. *Nonprofit and Voluntary Sector Quarterly, 42*(3), 584–602.

Anheier, H., & Salamon, L. M. (2006). The nonprofit sector in comparative perspective. In W. W. Powell & R. Steinberg (Eds.), *The nonprofit sector: A research handbook*, (2nd ed., pp. 89–116). New Haven, CT: Yale University Press.

Chen, C. A. (2012). Explaining the difference of work attitudes between public and nonprofit managers: The views of rule constraints and motivation styles. *The American Review of Public Administration, 42*(4), 437–460.

Collings, G. D., & Mellahi, K. (2009). Strategic talent management: A review and research agenda. *Human Resource Management Review, 19*, 304–313.

De Cooman, R., De Geiter, S., Pepermans, R., & Jegers M. (2011). A cross-sector comparison of motivation-related concepts in for-profit and not-for-profit service organizations. *Nonprofit and Voluntary Sector Quarterly, 40*(2), 296–317.

Devaro, J., & Brookshire, D. (2007). Promotions and incentives in nonprofit and for-profit organizations. *Industrial and Labor Relations Review, 60*, 311–339.

Garavan, T. N., Carbery, R., & Rock, A. (2012). Mapping talent development: Definition, scope and architecture. *European Journal of Training and Development, 36*(1), 5–24.

Giancola, F. L. (2011). Examining the job itself as a source of employee motivation. *Compensation & Benefits Review, 43*(1), 23–29.

Hiltrop, J. (1999). The quest for the best: Human resource practices to attract and retain talent. *European Management Journal, 17*(4), 422–430.

Kim, S., & McLean, G. (2012). Global talent management: Necessity, challenges, and the roles of HRD. *Advances in Developing Human Resources, 14*(4), 566–585.

Koch, D. J., Dreher, A., Nunnenkamp, P., & Thiele, R. (2009). Keeping a low profile: What determines the allocation of aid by non-governmental organizations? *World Development, 37*(5), 902–918.

Kucherov, D., & Zavyalova, E. (2012). HRD practices and talent management in the companies with the employer brand. *European Journal of Training and Development, 36*(1), 86–104.

Leete, L. (2000). Wage equity and employee motivation in nonprofit and for-profit organizations. *Journal of Economic Behavior & Organization, 34*, 423–446.

Lewis, D. (2003). Theorizing the organization and management of non-governmental development organizations: Towards a composite approach. *Public Management Review, 5*(3), 325–344.

Management Sciences for Health. (1998). *Human resource development (HRD): Assessment instrument for non-governmental organizations (NGOs) and public sector health organizations.* Retrieved from http://www.who.int/hrh/tools/hrd_instrument.pdf

Mann, G. A. (2006). A motive to serve: Public service motivation in human resource management and the role of PSM in the nonprofit sector. *Public Personnel Management, 35*, 33–48.

McCulloch, M. C., & Turban, D. B. (2007). Using person-organization fit to select employees for high-turnover jobs. *International Journal of Selection and Assessment, 15*(1), 63–71.

Mirvis, P. H., & Hackett, E. J. (1983). Work and work force characteristics in the nonprofit sector. *Monthly Labor Review, 106*(4), 3–12.

Najam, A. (2000). The four-C's of third sector—government relations: Cooperation, confrontation, complementarity, and co-optation. *Nonprofit Management and Leadership, 10*(4), 375–396.

Nilsson, S., & Ellström, P. (2012). Employability and talent management: Challenges for HRD practices. *European Journal of Training and Development, 36*(1), 26–45.

Perry, J. L., Mesch, D., & Paarlberg, L. (2006, July/August). Motivating employees in a new governance era: The performance paradigm revisited. *Public Administration Review,* 505–514.

Pink, D. H. (2009). *Drive: The surprising truth about what motivates us.* New York, NY: Riverhead Books.

Pruis, E. (2011). The five key principles for talent development. *Industrial and Commercial Training, 43*(4), 206–216.

Ronalds, P. (2010). *The change imperative: Creating the next generation NGO.* Sterling, VA: Kumarian Press.

Ryan, R. M., & Deci, E. L. (2000). Self-determination theory and the facilitation of intrinsic motivation, social development, and well-being. *American Psychologist, 55*(1), 68–78.

Salamon, L. M., & Anheier, H. K. (1997). *Defining the nonprofit sector: A cross-national analysis.* New York, NY: St. Martin Press.

Schepers, C., De Gieter, S., Pepermans, R., Du Bois, C., Caers, R., & Jegers, M. (2005). How are people of the non-profit sector motivated? A research need. *Nonprofit Management & Leadership, 16*, 191–208.

Vakil, A. (1997). Confronting the classification problem: Toward a taxonomy of NGOs. *World Development, 25*(12), 2057–2070.

Valentinov, V. (2007). The property rights approach to nonprofit organizations: The role of intrinsic motivation. *Public Organization Review, 7*, 41–55.

CHAPTER 7

TALENT DEVELOPMENT OF GLOBAL VIRTUAL TEAM LEADERS

Challenges and Strategies

Soo Jeoung Han, Shinhee Jeong, and Michael Beyerlein

In the era of globalization, workplaces around the world have become larger, more diverse, and more complicated (Briscoe, Schuler, & Claus, 2009). The advancement of technology has changed the way of working and the need for organizations to manage their workforces in a global context. Many employees have started to work internationally in virtual teams where they rely on the use of online technology tools. Virtual teams help business in many organizations by cutting costs (e.g., reduced office space and equipment), broadening the net of availability, and cooperating with qualified talent from all over the world. The ways that virtual teams provide and enhance the use of resources has been recognized in multinational companies for some time. Because of the economic, knowledge and technology gap between developing countries and economically advanced ones (Zhouying, 2005), virtual teams may provide a tool of special value for their smaller organizations.

Talent Development and the Global Economy:
Perspectives from Special Interest Groups, pp. 93–125
Copyright © 2017 by Information Age Publishing

In the war for talent, many organizations desire to recruit talented employees from all over the world. For example, multinational companies create international teams to pool global talent and meet organizational goals. However, due to the visa issue, long processes, travel expenses, and recruiting efforts, it is difficult to bring this talents on board. These constraints can be overcome by working virtually with highly skilled global experts dispersed around the globe.

Although virtual teams promise some benefits, national and cultural heterogeneity increases the complexity of employee relations, collaboration dynamics, and team performance beyond that of face-to-face teamwork settings (Pauleen, 2003b; Piri & Niinimaki, 2011). The national differences (e.g., language, cultural norms, values, working styles, etc.) among team members can cause conflict, miscommunication, and low team performance. Geographic dispersion and physical distances also disrupt daily workflow activities; therefore, effective leadership is necessary to bring multinational teams together for effective performance (Gibson & Gibbs, 2006).

These challenges suggest that organizations may need to prepare their managers and team members for working in different types of teams (McDonough, Kahn, & Barczak, 2001), and in teams where members speak several different languages and come from a variety of cultures. As a result, the notion of a global workforce and global virtual teams has received extensive attention recently from scholars (e.g., Briscoe, Schuler, & Claus, 2009; Collings, Scullion, & Dowling, 2009; Gibson & Cohen, 2003).

Successfully building and leading virtual teams involves talent development. Specifically, the key to the success of global work is leadership. Leadership development tools can be helpful for improving team and organizational effectiveness. In this chapter, we have identified several challenges of global virtual team processes and present several strategies on how global virtual team leaders can overcome those challenges. There is value in creating talent development activities to meet those challenges (Beechler & Woodward, 2009; Collings & Mellahi, 2009).

We define talent development as the process of changing an organization, its employees, its stakeholders, team leaders, and groups of people within it by using planned and unplanned learning in order to achieve a competitive advantage for the organization. Deliberate attention to talent development is essential because the greatest challenge multinational organizations face today involves aligning expertise with projects and problems across national borders. Management and leaders face challenges in encouraging global virtual team members to share resources, transfer knowledge, and work collaboratively because meeting organizational goals and implementing complex business strategies can generate conflict (Snow, Snell, Davison, & Hambrick, 1996). Understanding basic team process challenges is a necessary first step for exploring the impact of leadership on a multinational team.

Therefore, our purpose has been to explore the process factors that disable global virtual team (GVT) processes and identify the strategies that global virtual team leaders can use to develop GVTs. We also explored the possibilities and strategies to develop the global virtual team leaders (GVTL).

GLOBAL VIRTUAL TEAM PROCESS AND GLOBAL VIRTUAL TEAM LEADERSHIP

Development of capability for the GVT requires attention to multiple forms of talent and the support systems surrounding the teams. Here we focus only on the development of team leadership, a process that is embedded in the larger talent development system and a capability that provides crucial inputs into the development of the team itself. A larger body of literature exists that is focused on team development, although only a small but growing segment of it focuses on GVTs. There is a paucity of literature that is focused on the development of GVTLs. In addition to most of the competencies required by leaders in face-to-face situations, GVTLs require some unique capabilities because of their work with GVTs. In this section, we define GVTs and present a team process framework. We also have identified GVT leadership competencies.

Definition of Global Virtual Teams

The distinctive feature of a virtual team is the reliance on information technology as the primary form of communication (Powell, Piccoli, & Ives, 2004). Since global teams include members from different countries and are typically culturally diverse (Powell et al., 2004), researchers have typically studied global teams in a virtual setting (e.g., Jarvenpaa & Leidner, 1998; Kayworth & Leidner, 2000; Maznevski & Chudoba, 2000). Global teams, as defined by Maloney and Zellmer-Bruhn (2006), differ from other teams in two ways: (a) a globally dispersed work environment, and (b) heterogeneity on multiple dimensions. Several researchers have focused exclusively on global virtual teams (e.g., Hardin, Fuller, & Davison, 2007; Jarvenpaa, & Leidner, 1999; Kayworth & Leidner, 2002; Klitmøller, & Lauring, 2013; Maznevski & Chudoba, 2000).

As more teams interact virtually, there has been an increase in definitions of virtual teams (VTs). VTs generally consist of geographically and/ or organizationally dispersed members who work toward a shared goal by using various kinds of technologies for communication (Ale, Ahmed, & Taha, 2009). Hertel, Geiser, and Konradt (2005) noted a VT relies on media interaction (e.g., chat, e-mail, audio conference, and video conferencing) for members to interact with one another in place of meeting face-to-face. Most definitions of VTs include two dimensions of context, such as geography and time (Kayworth & Leidner, 2000; Montoya-Weiss, Massey, & Song, 2001) or geographic dispersion and electronic dependence (Cohen & Gibson, 2003). However, more scholars have expanded their conceptual framework of VTs by including other dimensions, such as the level of technology support, degree of time working apart on task, and degree of physical distance (Kirkman & Mathieu, 2005).

Scholars recently added cultural diversity as one of the defining characteristics of global VTs (e.g., Chen, Kirkman, Kim, Farh, & Tangirala, 2010; Gibson & Gibbs, 2006; Martins, Gilson, & Maynard, 2004). Martins, Gilson, and Maynard (2004) suggested four dimensions: geographical dispersion, use of computer-mediated communication, temporality, and diversity. Based on this evolving view of virtuality, we adopt a GVT concept followed by Baba, Gluesing, Ratner, and Wagner (2004), because the teams involve the components of national cultural diversity, physical and temporal distance, interdependence, and reliance on technology.

In this chapter, we focus on national cultural diversity. Culture is a multilevel team composition variable ranging from organizational culture to national culture that can impact the team processes (Dreo, Kunkel, & Mitchell, 2002). Many scholars had difficulty defining culture because it consists of many implicit and explicit elements, such as behaviors, values, norms, and basic assumptions (Groeschl & Doherty, 2000). Specifically, national culture is defined as the collective mindset that distinguishes members of one nation from another (Hoftede, Hofstede, & Minkov, 2010)—a form of tacit knowledge (Nonaka & Takeuchi, 1995) that natives know and nonnatives can usually only know about. For national cultural diversity in global and distributed teams, prior researchers have recognized language and country of residence as two critical components of culture (Staples & Zhao, 2006; Vignovic & Thompson, 2010).

Team Processes Framework

In this section, we present a GVT framework involving the following four processes (see Figure 7.1): (a) behavior, (b) affective, (c) motivational, and (d) cognitive. Team process researchers have distinguished cognitive, affective-motivational, and behavioral functions as keys to team effectiveness by enabling team members to combine their resources to resolve task demands (Kozlowski & Ilgen, 2006). To facilitate team processes, shared group identity emerges when team members have a sense of (a) a behavior component of joint effort, (b) an affective component of emotional attraction, (c) a motivational component of effort toward a common goal, and (d) cognitive component of belonging and knowledge sharing (Zaccaro, Rittman, & Marks, 2001) as shown in Figure 7.1. The four components of the framework represent a number of processes that overlap to capture some of the complexity of the GVT phenomenon.

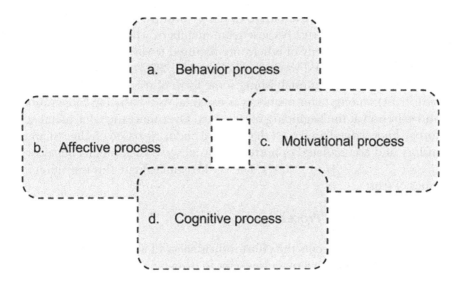

Figure 7.1.   GVT Process Framework.

Team Behavior Process

Team behavior processes refer to the actions performed by team members to achieve a common goal (Salas & Cannon-Bowers, 2000; Shuffler). Successful virtual teams share several common behaviors among team members such as task-related communication (Kanawattanachai & Yoo, 2007; Shachaf, 2008), decision making (Chiu & Staples, 2013; Shachaf, 2008), and conflict resolution (Montoya-Weiss et al., 2001; Mortensen & Hinds, 2001; Paul, Samarah, Seetharaman, & Mykytyn Jr, 2004). These behaviors are typically developed by leaders, so it is important for leaders to facilitate the onset of effective behaviors.

Team Affective Process

Team affective processes refer to the socioemotional states such as trust, group emotions, interpersonal liking, or group cohesiveness as part of the emotional climate of the group (Barsade & Gibson, 2012; Gully, Devine, & Whitney, 2012; Kasper-Fuehrer & Ashkanasy, 2001). For example, team affective functions can be represented in terms of perceived team support, which is related to building trust and team cohesion (Kasper-Fuehrer & Ashkanasy, 2001). However, the results of case studies suggest that trust appears to be fragile and temporary in GVTs (Jarvenpaa & Leidner, 1998; Jarvenpaa, Knoll, & Leidner, 1998; Polzer, Crisp, Jarvenpaa, & Kim, 2006). Virtual teams are known to develop "swift trust" rather than cognitive- or affect-based trust because team members, who have not yet built confidence in the ability of others, are required to suspend uncertainty to achieve the established work goals (Germain, 2011). Crisp and Jarvenpaa (2013), noted that establishing some form of trust immediately (e.g., swift trust) among team members is essential as a basis for cooperation and cohesion at the beginning of a project. Over time, the GVT members form a knowledge-based trust that is more enduring based on their shared history and accumulated opportunities to observe each other's behaviors (Robert, Denis, & Hung, 2009). The GVTL can facilitate this transition in types of trust.

Team Motivational Process

Motivation represents the effort individuals will invest in a task. At the team level, motivational processes refer to team members' shared commitment to their shared goals which impacts the team's capacity to perform successfully (Kozlowski & Ilgen, 2006). Teams with strong beliefs about their abilities can achieve higher performance levels since they put more effort toward the task (Gully, Incalcaterra, Joshi, & Beaubien, 2002). The development of a collective motivational process in a GVT setting may be challenging since they lack time for team building and interactions.

Team Cognitive Process

Most virtual teams do knowledge work by sharing knowledge, learning from each other, and co-creating solutions to problems. Team cognitive processes refer to the importance of knowledge in team functioning (DeChurch & Mesmer-Magnus, 2010). Knowledge sharing and experience that guides effective teamwork is a key to the cognitive process (Shuffler, DiazGranados, & Salas, 2011). Cognitive functioning can also be represented in terms of team learning (Edmondson, 1999; Edmondson, Bohmer, & Pisano, 2001). Shared mental models emphasize knowledge or understanding that members have in common, which contribute to the team's performance (Kozlowski & Ilgen, 2006). Shared mental models develop over time and serve as lenses all the members can use to make sense of information related to project goals.

To sum up, leaders need to pay attention to team process and deliberately monitor the development of team behavior, affective, motivational, and cognitive processes. Team performance directly relates to a leader's responsibility (Kayworth & Leidner, 2002; Zaccaro et al., 2001).

Global Virtual Team Leadership Capabilities

The advent and rapid advance of communication and information technology have accelerated the process of globalization and forced organizations to deal with cyberspace as an emerging workplace and operate with virtual teams globally. There are great advantages of virtual teams such as the borderless recruitment of the best talented members and efficient product development due to nonstop working schedules around the world (Davis & Bryant, 2003). For example, a virtual team with members located around the globe can hand off the project work at the end a work day in one time zone to the members just beginning their work day in another time zone. However, virtual teams also have to deal with multiple hurdles including communication, trust-building, scheduling, and technological problems (Kayworth & Leidner, 2002). Moreover, given the characteristics coming from the global context, such as dispersion of geography, time, culture, and language, GVTs are challenged with more complex problems that often result in lower individual commitment, team satisfaction, and increased social loafing (Kahai, Sosik, & Avolio, 2003; Kayworth & Leidner, 2002).

To overcome these issues and increase the effectiveness of GVTs, leadership has received substantial attention as a key determinant of team performance (Davis & Bryant, 2003; Kayworth & Leidner, 2002; Pauleen, 2003a). Leaders possess the power of mobilizing organizational resources, changing the organizational culture and climate, and promoting individuals' behavioral changes (Rondinelli & Heffron, 2009). Leaders make the difference in team performance as they facilitate members' engagement in teamwork processes (Cascio & Shurygailo, 2003). Moreover, from a sociotechnical systems approach, leaders play a pivotal role in aligning and bridging gaps between technological, environmental, and social systems, which impact organizational success (Avolio, Kahai, & Dodge, 2001).

Regardless of a virtual or collocated team setting, every leader may share similar roles or responsibilities to perform, which are traditionally categorized as task-oriented or relationship-oriented behaviors (Kayworth & Leidner, 2002; Yukl, Gordon, & Taber, 2002). However, virtual team leaders face additional and unique challenges in implementing those responsibilities as they have limited opportunity for face-to-face interaction with team members and access to their social clues (Brake, 2006; Malhotra, Majchrzak & Rosen, 2007). GVTLs must sense and determine what actions/interventions need to be conducted through electronic communication, and so face greater uncertainty about effective responses. Moreover, it is challenging for virtual team leaders to establish the sense of their presence (i.e., telepresence) to team members in an electronic context, whereas traditional team leaders can do that easily by just physically being there (Zigurs, 2003). With these reasons, Avolio and colleagues (2001) argued that advanced information technology has created a new context that changes the nature of leadership. They also utilized the term *e-leadership* to describe leadership in virtual teams and defined it as "a social influence process mediated by advanced information technology to produce a change in attitudes, feelings, thinking, behavior, and/or performance with individuals, groups, and/ or organizations" (p. 617).

A substantial amount of literature has attempted to address leadership capabilities or strategies required to lead a GVT effectively. In one of the most comprehensive models for GVT leadership, Davis and Bryant (2003) presented behaviors for leading GVTs across organizational, team, dyad, and individual levels. They also discussed the model through Full Range Leadership (i.e., laissez-faire leadership, transactional leadership, and transformational leadership) and through communication and collaboration technology, knowledge management, culture, and the team life cycle. GVTLs need a multilevel perspective. For example, at organizational level, Davis and Bryant emphasized integrated and consistent organizational factors such as reward systems, goal setting, and performance appraisal for GVTs across functional and geographical boundaries. They also analyzed team, dyadic (e.g., leader-member exchange theory), and individual (e.g., distributed leadership) levels of leadership. They reported laissez-faire leadership to be less effective than transactional leadership and transformational leadership in the context of leading virtual teams. Leaders have to choose various tools, either synchronous or asynchronous, considering information richness, social presence, and implementation, as well as work to promote team learning. Leadership must adjust to the needs of the team as it changes throughout its life cycle. Lastly, leaders should be aware of the influence of culture as it permeates and interacts with every aspect and process of leadership, team processes, and performance.

Even though Kayworth and Leidner (2002) indicated a high similarity of leadership capabilities between virtual and traditional face-to-face teams (i.e., task-oriented, relationship-oriented) from the behavioral perspective of leadership, they argued that the emphasis of certain roles may differ in virtual settings, supported by the contingency and situational leadership perspective. Specifically, communication and social facilitation capabilities are more valued in a virtual team. Also, they accentuated the importance of behavioral complexity as effective leaders often perform contradicting and competing role behaviors. For example, subordinates may perceive a leader to be effective when he or she demonstrates authoritative behaviors, but being empathetic at the same time.

Mukherjee, Lahiri, Mukherjee, and Billing (2012) suggested cognitive, social, behavioral capabilities from the perspective of transactional and transformational leadership differ across five stages of a team's life cycle (i.e., preparations, launch, performance management, team development, and disbanding). They defined cognitive capabilities as abilities to reflect, analyze, and synthesize information; social capabilities as interpersonal skills and social manner; and behavioral capabilities as enablers of influencing others to think and function. For example, at the preparation stage, leaders utilize their judgmental skills to plan and design virtual teams, relying on cognitive leadership capabilities rather than social and behavioral capabilities.

In summary, despite the current criticism by some scholars that virtual team leadership capabilities are similar to those for traditional teams, we argue e-leadership is different in important ways. Virtual teams present a unique situation or context where leaders must consider technology availability, culture, time/geographic differences, and team life cycle. In the following section, we will focus on identifying process inhibitors of virtual teams in the literature and suggest relevant leadership strategies to overcome such problems.

CHALLENGES OF GLOBAL VIRTUAL TEAM PROCESSES

In this section, we explore the process factors that can disable GVT learning and performance. Then, we provide specific suggestions for how GVT leaders address these components by facilitating each process.

Although GVTs enable companies to combine skills, talents, and other advantages from people across the globe, national and cultural heterogeneity in virtual teams adds more complexity to employee relations, collaboration dynamics, and team performance (Pauleen, 2004). GVT literature reveals inconsistent effects for cultural diversity across different contexts with both positive and negative impacts (Shachaf, 2008). People typically interpret information based on their cultural values and biases, which leads to misinterpretations (Pauleen, 2004). Perceived differences in national cultures can lead to unhealthy stereotypes in GVTs (Au & Marks, 2012). The challenges of virtual assignments are caused by the inability of partners to interact due to national cultural differences (e.g., interpretation problems, insufficient language skills, and a different context), more than by the insufficient manageability of technical systems (Holtbrügge & Schillo, 2011). For example, technical language violations (e.g., spelling and grammatical errors) in e-mail have been shown to form negative perceptions regarding agreeableness and trustworthiness (Vignovic & Thompson, 2010). Therefore, cultural diversity of linguistic and national factors can create weaknesses and result in both task and relationship conflict in the global VTs (Kankanhalli, Tan, & Wei, 2007).

In Table 7.1, we identify GVT process challenges by synthesizing 60 empirical GVT studies. As mentioned in the previous section, we categorize each process factor into four processes: (a) behavior, (b) motivation, (c) affective, and (d) cognitive process. Each GVT process is broken into several process factors which are then tied directly to challenges identified in the cited literature. Clearly, there are a number of issues for the GVTL to consider in developing an effective GVT. There is little evidence in the literature to suggest that GVTLs typically receive training related to these challenges.

Strategies for Global Virtual Team Leaders

In Table 7.2, we identified GVTL strategies to overcome GVT process challenges by synthesizing 60 empirical GVT studies. As mentioned in the previous section, we categorize GVT leader's strategies into three levels: (a) behavior, (b) social, and (c) cognitive strategies.

Table 7.2 clearly shows that GVTLs have a number of options in dealing with virtual team process challenges. In the short term, the list of strategies might be used as a checklist for GVTLs or their coaches to determine how to address specific challenges and how to build leadership capability. In the long term, the list can guide creation of a curriculum for leadership talent development to increase success in virtual environments.

SOLUTIONS AND RECOMMENDATIONS

The number of virtual teams is rapidly increasing as virtual teams play an important role in strengthening organizational flexibility and competitiveness of growing importance (Malhotra et al., 2007; Pauleen, 2003b; Zigurs, 2003). As a result, organizations pay more attention to developing and preparing future leaders who understand the dynamics of virtual teams and possess appropriate skills and knowledge in leading virtual teams (Rosen, Furst, & Blackburn, 2006). However, Rosen et al. (2006) pointed out that the importance of virtual team leadership development is underestimated and failed to obtain sympathy from top management. For this reason, only a small number of organizations provide such training programs, and it is highly doubtful about their quality and effectiveness (Malhotra et al., 2007; Rosen et al., 2006).

Table 7.1.   GVT Process Challenges

GVT Processes	Process Factors	GVT Challenges	Reference
Behavior process	Communicating	-GVTs can cause communication problem, task conflict, and misunderstanding. -Fostering effective communication among GVTs is more challenging than it is in collocated or virtual teams. -GVT requires early and frequent task-oriented communication -Ethnic diversity leads to more informal and open communication in the teams.	Chang et al., 2011; Chiu & Staples, 2013; Johansson et al., 1999; Kanawattanachai & Yoo, 2007; Kankanhalli et al., 2006; Kayworth & Leidner, 2000; McDonough et al., 2001; Monalisa et al., 2008; Oertig & Buergi, 2006; Shachaf, 2005; Shachaf, 2008; Suchan & Hayzak, 2001; Van Ryssen & Godar, 2000
	Initiating task	- GVT may contribute to task conflict. - Differences in cultural values, practices, and organizations impacted how the project task viewed, what knowledge was valued, and the recognition of an individual's contributions to the project.	Jarvenpaa & Keating, 2011; Kankanhalli et al., 2007
	Coordinating	- GVT process hinders coordination due to power, culture, and communication. - GVT experiences issues with keeping on schedule and staying on budget. - GVT requires thoughtful selection of communication media due to different preferences.	Johansson et al., 1999; Kayworth & Leidner, 2000; Maznevski & Chudoba, 2001; McDonough et al., 2001; Van Ryssen & Godar, 2000
	Using collaborative technology	- GVT faces challenges of managing virtual aspects of communication. -Using collaborative technology hinders trust building. - GVT can reduce team process losses associated with stereotyping, personality conflicts, power, politics, and critiques commonly experienced by face-to-face teams. - GVT should improve language accuracy and mitigate intercultural miscommunication resulting from verbal differences among team members, and eliminates nonverbal differences by using e-mail.	Kirkman et al., 2002; Oertig & Buergi, 2006; Shachaf, 2005; Staples & Zhao, 2006

(Table continues on next page)

Table 7.1.   Continued

GVT Processes	Process Factors	GVT Challenges	Reference
Motivational process	Goal-setting	- GVTs face greater challenges in ensuring that project goals remain stable.	Gatlin-Watts et al., 2007; McDonough et al., 2001
	Norming	- GVT finds difficulties in norming due to various standards of acceptable behavior and cultural norms. - GVT faces challenges to establish expectations around knowledge sharing due to in-group/out-group dynamics.	Fain & Kline, 2013; Gibson & Gibbs, 2006; Krumm et al., 2013; McDonough et al., 2001
	Sharing identity	- GVTs need to build shared identity as it is associated with less task conflict. - A strong sense of belonging to the global culture share their emotional norms strongly. - Strong norms enable the emergence of a global identity. - Individuals from different cultures are likely to show more agreement on the proper display norms for both positive and negative emotions for GVTs rather than culturally homogeneous virtual teams.	Glikson & Erez, 2013; Mortensen & Hinds, 2001

(Table continues on next page)

Table 7.1.   Continued

GVT Processes	Process Factors	GVT Challenges	Reference
Affective process	Promoting cohesion	- People tend to have relationship conflict due to cultural diversity. - GVT members face challenges in developing interpersonal relationships due to the lack of shared beliefs/experiences.	Daniel et al., 2013; Glikson & Erez, 2013; Kankanhalli et al., 2006; Lurey & Raisinghani, 2001 ; McDonough et al., 2001; Newell et al., 2007; Ocker et al., 2011; Pauleen, 2003b; Van Ryssen & Godar, 2000
	Building trust	- GVT shares few informal messages or little social information, which can reduce trust. - GVT members relies more on a cognitive than an affective element of trust.	Connaughton & Daly, 2004; Holtbrügge et al., 2011; Jarvenpaa & Leidner, 1999; Kanawattanachai & Yoo, 2002; Kirkman et al., 2002; McDonough et al., 2001; Oertig & Buergi, 2006; Peters & Karren, 2009; Pinjani & Palvia, 2013
	Understanding cultural differences	- GVT members holds unhealthy racial and national stereotypes. - GVT members shares little social information due to cultural differences. - GVT engages conflict due to in-group/out-group dynamics.	Anawati & Craig, 2006; Au & Marks, 2012; Fain & Kline, 2013; McDonough et al., 2001; Mortensen & Hinds, 2001; Newell et al., 2007; Berg, 2012; Chiu & Staples, 2013; Gibson & Gibbs, 2006; Panteli & Davison , 2005; Polzer et al., 2006

(Table continues on next page)

Table 7.1. Continued

GVT Processes	Process Factors	GVT Challenges	Reference
Cognitive process	Decision making	- GVT impairs decision process quality. - When GVTs follow a collaborative conflict management style, the performance of the team seems to improve regarding decision process satisfaction, perceived decision quality, and degree of group agreement.	Chiu & Staples, 2013; Paul et al., 2004
	Intercultural learning	- GVT results in intercultural misunderstandings. - GVT members bring conflicts due to communication style differences. - GVT impairs decision quality.	Anawati & Craig, 2006; Fain & Kline, 2013; Gibson & Gibbs, 2006; Glikson & Erez, 2013; Hardin et al., 2007; Holtbrügge et al., 2011; Jarvenpaa & Keating, 2011; Mockaitis et al., 2012; Monalisa et al., 2008; Mortensen & Hinds, 2001; Paul et al., 2005; Shachaf, 2008; Umans, 2008
	Knowledge sharing	- GVT faces difficulties in keeping project goals stable. - GVT members hinder information flow due to in-group/out-group perceptions and cultural differences. - GVT causes uneven distribution of information due to differences in the salience of information among members and relative differences in speed of access to information.	Cramton, 2001; Gibson & Gibbs, 2006; Newell et al., 2007; Pinjani & Palvia, 2013; Robey, Khoo, & Powers, 2000; Umans, 2008

Table 7.2.   Global Virtual Teams Strategies

GVT Process Factors	Strategies for GVT Leaders			Publication (supporting research)
	Leader's Behavior Strategies	*Leader's Social Strategies*	*Leader's Cognitive Strategies*	
Facilitate task-related communication	- Leaders should encourage team members to adapt and attempt to change their behavior in both spoken and written communication. - GVT leaders should use various communication methods to be satisfied and be successful.	- Creating a psychologically safe communication climate is needed. - Task-related communication appears to be necessary to maintain trust.	- Effective leadership associated with ability to foster structure that help communication effectiveness, communication satisfaction, role clarity, better relational skills.	Anawati & Craig, 2006; Gibson & Gibbs, 2006; Holtbrügge et al., 2011; Jarvenpaa et al., 1998; Kayworth & Leidner, 2000; Kayworth & Leidner, 2002
Initiating task	- Increasing the volume and frequency of task-oriented communication in the initial phase of the project is a significant determinant of team performance.	- It is effective to apply a supportive rather than directive management style.	- Leaders should provide immediate feedback.	Kanawattanachai & Yoo, 2007; Kankanhalli et al., 2007; Vogel et al., 2001

(Table continues on next page)

Table 7.2.   (Continued)

GVT Process Factors	Strategies for GVT Leaders			Publication (supporting research)
	Leader's Behavior Strategies	Leader's Social Strategies	Leader's Cognitive Strategies	
Coordinating	- Communication should be increased to improve coordination process. -Leaders should provide a variety of options for communication medias rather than specially designed coordinating technologies. - Regular face-to-face meeting should be provided for necessary coordination.	- Leaders must assist the team in bridging the distance faultline because the optimal leadership configuration depends upon distance considerations.	- GVTL need to understand that successful enactment of temporal coordination mechanisms is associated with higher performance; the influence of coordination on interaction behaviors affects performance.	Ocker et al., 2011; Massey et al., 2003; Maznevski & Chudoba, 2001; Robey et al., 2000

(Table continues on next page)

Table 7.2.   (Continued)

| GVT Process Factors | Strategies for GVT Leaders | | | Publication (supporting research) |
	Leader's Behavior Strategies	Leader's Social Strategies	Leader's Cognitive Strategies	
Use effective communication technology	- Leaders should be supportive with communication technology and information. - GVTLs need to know that cultural diversity influences selection of the communication media. - Leaders need to select the appropriate communication media according to the given task and cultural context they work in ("netiquette").	- Leaders need to help team members communicate social and emotional information, not only task-related information. -Achieving an appropriate balance between technological and personal support is crucial in guiding virtual teams to successful results.	- Training on how to communicate and how to use technology can be helpful.	Gareis, 2006; Gavidia et al.,[5] 2004; Holtbrügge et al., 2011; Monalisa et al., 2008; Shachaf, 2008; Van Ryssen & Godar, 2000; Vogel et al., 2001
Goal-setting	- Leaders should balance individual control with shared objectives and bring out common goals. -GVTLs should promote a common goal and value.	- Leaders should help members to establish trust and cooperation to adhere to explicit rules.	- Leaders should provide training to facilitate learning about the cultural norms and values of their respective counterparts. - GVT needs to embody the knowledge, skills, abilities related to working conscientiously to overcome the challenges.	Au & Marks, 2012; Gatlin-Watts et al., 2007; Holtbrügge et al., 2011; Krumm et al., 2013; Sivunen, 2006

(Table continues on next page)

Table 7.2.   (Continued)

GVT Process Factors	Strategies for GVT Leaders			Publication (supporting research)
	Leader's Behavior Strategies	Leader's Social Strategies	Leader's Cognitive Strategies	
Norming	- GVTLs need to establish norms around communication patterns. - Adhere to explicit rules and self-disciplined proactive work behaviors are required to ensure trust, cooperation, cohesion, and performance. - Creating common ground helps.	- Establishing a communication behavior in the first few keystrokes is needed to maintain trust. - GVT needs to display the proper norms for both positive and negative emotions.	- A training should be implemented to facilitate learning about the cultural norms and values of their respective counterparts.	Glikson & Erez, 2013; Holtbrügge et al., 2011; Jarvenpaa & Leidner, 1998; Kirkman et al., 2002; Krumm et al., 2013; Vogel et al., 2001
Sharing identity	- Frequent monitoring of the progress of the teams is helpful.	- Regarding affective conflict, a shared identity may help teams to better manage conflict. - Team leaders need to monitor subgroup development carefully to ensure that a sense of team identity and coherence is maintained and to prevent a them-and-us attitude.		Mortensen & Hinds, 2001; Panteli & Davison, 2005; Vogel et al., 2001

(Table continues on next page)

Table 7.2.   (Continued)

GVT Process Factors	Strategies for GVT Leaders			Publication (supporting research)
	Leader's Behavior Strategies	Leader's Social Strategies	Leader's Cognitive Strategies	
Promoting cohesion	- Leaders need to give lot of time for the team work and be able to build higher-level management support for one's team. - Stimulating interaction from the start face-to-face (sandwich structure) helps establish social bonds and relationships.	- Team leadership play important roles in reinforcing timeliness and consistency of team interaction. - Both friendship and engagement can be enhanced by increase the time spent on the task and the duration of the project. - Having richer communication facilitates socialization.	- Implement training to standardize knowledge across the team and to develop a common basis for collaboration. -Mentoring program enables socialization of members.	Cordery et al., 2009; Crossman & Bordia, 2011; Holtbrügge et al., 2011; Kayworth & Leidner, 2000; Kirkman et al., 2002; Robey et al., 2000; Sivunen, 2006; Staples & Zhao, 2006; Suchan & Hayzak, 2001; Vogel et al., 2001

(Table continues on next page)

Table 7.2.   (Continued)

GVT Process Factors	Strategies for GVT Leaders			Publication (supporting research)
	Leader's Behavior Strategies	Leader's Social Strategies	Leader's Cognitive Strategies	
Building trust	- Exchanging social and informal messages is needed to maintain positive atmosphere and trust within the team. - Early and frequent task-oriented communication play a critical role in forming the initial beliefs and trust of team members about each other's specialized knowledge. - Face-to-face meetings needed to gain respect, trust, and interpersonal relations.	- Leaders need to develop trust and respect to enable member to successfully interact with each other. - Leaders need to develop trust and respect to enable member to successfully interact with each other and provide each other with what they need to develop the product. - Interpersonal skills may be more important than task-related skills as team members attempt to communicate effectively without relying on non-verbal cues. - Emphasis on relationship building in multiple boundary crossing teams is needed.	- Leaders should give positive feedback. -Training and coaching are essential in achieving mutual understanding and trust. - GVTLs should understand the presence of swift trust.	Dekker et al., 2008; Gatlin-Watts et al., 2007; Gavidia et al., 2004; Jarvenpaa & Leidner, 1999; Jarvenpaa & Leidner,[12] 1998; Kanawattanachai & Yoo, 2002; Kirkman et al., 2002; Lurey & Raisinghani, 2001; Monalisa et al., 2008; Oertig & Buergi, 2006; Pauleen, 2003a; Sivunen, 2006; Suchan & Hayzak, 2001

(Table continues on next page)

Table 7.2.   (Continued)

GVT Process Factors	Strategies for GVT Leaders			Publication (supporting research)
	Leader's Behavior Strategies	Leader's Social Strategies	Leader's Cognitive Strategies	
Understanding cultural differences	- The negative effects of cultural differences can be minimized by introducing diversity. - Leaders should help team members adapt and attempt to change their behavior in allowing for religious beliefs and time zone differences to improve process.	- GVTLs should promote a common goal and value. -GVTLs need special care on the cultural aspects of team forming, as different perceptions of team members can have a relevant effect on the outcome of the team process. - GVTLs need to create a psychologically safe communication climate.	- GVT needs to remove cultural barrier and adapt to the new culture. - Leaders should recognize that people come from different cultural backgrounds, and they have different workforce structures at different sides that have different mindsets. - GVTL should understand different orientation of the members because it influences its collaborative conflict management style. -A different management skill set should be developed to deal with the cultural and language complexities.	Anawati & Craig, 2006; Au & Marks, 2012; Chang et al., 2011; Cordery et al., 2009; Fain & Kline, 2013; Gavidia et al., 2004; Gibson & Gibbs, 2006; McDonough et al., 2001; Paul et al., 2005

(Table continues on next page)

Table 7.2.   (Continued)

GVT Process Factors	Strategies for GVT Leaders			Publication (supporting research)
	Leader's Behavior Strategies	Leader's Social Strategies	Leader's Cognitive Strategies	
Decision making	- Leaders should be supportive with communication technology and information.	- A psychologically safe communication climate should be created - GTVLs should help reduce relational conflicts. -Emotional display norms (greater expression of positive emotions and suppression of negative emotions) needed to be established.		Gibson & Gibbs, 2006; Glikson & Erez, 2013; Shachaf, 2008

(Table continues on next page)

Table 7.2.   (Continued)

GVT Process Factors	Strategies for GVT Leaders			Publication (supporting research)
	Leader's Behavior Strategies	Leader's Social Strategies	Leader's Cognitive Strategies	
Intercultural learning	- Leaders should encourage team members to adapt and attempt to change their behavior in both spoken and written communication. - Effective technologies for intercultural communication included e-mail, teleconferencing combined with e-meetings, and team room should be supported. - GVTLs should help members to actively experience intercultural learning to gain understanding of cross-cultural differences and honed their intercultural communication skills. - Increase communication can improve cultural understanding.	- GVT should create a friendly atmosphere that would facilitate learning. - Emotional and social factors in learning should be included.	- GVTLs should develop a different management skill set to deal with the cultural and language complexities. - A training should be implemented to facilitate learning about the cultural norms and values of members' respective counterparts.	Anawati & Craig, 2006; Crossman & Bordia, 2011; Gareis, 2006; Holtbrügge et al., 2011; McDonough et al., 2001; Robey et al., 2000; Shachaf, 2008

(Table continues on next page)

Table 7.2.   (Continued)

GVT Process Factors	Strategies for GVT Leaders			Publication (supporting research)
	Leader's Behavior Strategies	Leader's Social Strategies	Leader's Cognitive Strategies	
Knowledge sharing	- Efforts should be made at thinning team boundaries and facilitating information flows. - Reward system can support information-sharing.	- Leaders should create a psychologically safe communication climate for members to share their knowledge.	- Leaders should help members reduce in-group and out-group way of thinking. - Through different combinations of remote and face-to-face communication, using a variety of communication media, the learning of work practices became situated in the virtual community rather than imposed by managers or specially designed coordinating technologies.	Gibson & Gibbs, 2006; Holtbrügge et al., 2011, Robey et al., 2000; Suchan & Hayzak, 2001; Workman, 2007

Obstacles threatening virtual team success and relevant leadership strategies coping with those challenges identified in the previous section provide valuable insights for human resource practitioners, trainers, and virtual team leaders. First, leadership development programs for GVTs should be developed based on content for delivering unique skills and knowledge necessary for leading GVTs. In Table 7.2, we have provided a number of leadership behavioral, social, cognitive strategies to guide those content decisions. For example, to address communication technology problems, leaders must have a good understanding of effective online communication skills and how to select the most appropriate, comfortable, and agile communication media, given to assigned tasks and cultural contexts. Depending on topics for the content, organizations can design and develop such courses utilizing either internal or external experts. Furthermore, various training delivery methods can be considered such as action learning, simulation, or role playing. Pauleen (2003a) discussed action learning as a useful learning intervention as it allows working on real problems in virtual teams by reflecting on individuals' leadership experiences and sharing best practices. Additionally, assessment of training effectiveness should be systematically planned, which focuses on measuring actual performance improvement among trainees.

Second, human resource practitioners can make efforts to build organizational environment supportive of virtual teams utilizing various interventions such as mentoring, rewards, performance appraisal, or recognition. Moreover, in addition to formal training, organizations should also provide informal learning opportunities to develop related skills and knowledge, integrated with everyday work. Above all, it is imperative to communicate with top management and convince them of the importance of virtual team development and its unique challenges.

Third, technology literacy is becoming more essential. Communication technologies continue to become more sophisticated and to rapidly evolve. However, it is important for virtual team leaders to be aware that a new tool is not a panacea to solve all problems. Zigurs (2003) accentuated "appropriate application of tools to well-understood and well-managed work practices" (p. 348). GVTs should utilize an entire suite of communication tools. In choosing an e-tool for a specific task, leaders should consider various aspects such as accessibility and vividness and interactivity of media to ensure a leader's telepresence.

Finally, HR practitioners can work with managers to create effective selection systems for identifying people who can become effective at leading virtual teams when members represent a variety of cultures. Some people who are experts in technology or science, may not be able to easily develop the competencies and mindsets that effective VTs require.

Academically, further discussion to discover consequences of the interactions between leadership and technology is necessary. Avolio et al. (2001) argued that technology has transformed the leadership system, as well as the social system. Organizational culture and power structure also influence the interaction process. The relationships between virtual team leadership and corporate culture, policies, and team structure, as well as understanding leadership processes within context, also remain as essential questions for investigation (Avolio et al., 2001).

Another future research avenue may be to suggest a wide array of competencies in terms of traits, mindsets, knowledge, and skills in order to be an effective GVT leader. Competency refers to "an underlying characteristic of an individual that is causally related to criterion-referenced effective and/or superior performance" (Spencer & Spencer, 1993, p. 9). Competency-based approaches have been utilized to foster future leaders and develop high-performing and effective leaders in HR practice (Brownell & Goldsmith, 2006).

GVTs have become an essential way of organizing knowledge workers across the globe. The use of VTs will continue to expand. Effectiveness of GVTs depends on the effectiveness of the team leaders. They will need significant development opportunities to handle the challenges.

REFERENCES

Ale Ebrahim, N., Ahmed, S., & Taha, Z. (2009). Virtual R&D teams in small and medium enterprises: A literature review. *Scientific Research and Essays, 4*, 1575–1590.

Anawati, D., & Craig, A. (2006). Behavioral adaptation within cross-cultural virtual teams. *IEEE Transactions on Professional Communication, 49*(1), 44–56. doi:10.1109/TPC.2006.870459

Au, Y., & Marks, A. (2012). Virtual teams are literally and metaphorically invisible: Forging identity in culturally diverse virtual teams. *Employee Relations, 34*, 271–287. doi:10.1108/01425451211217707

Avolio, B. J., Kahai, S., & Dodge, G. E. (2000). E-leadership. *The Leadership Quarterly, 11*(4), 615–668. doi:10.1016/s1048-9843(00)00062-x

Baba, M. L., Gluesing, J., Ratner, H., & Wagner, K. H. (2004). The contexts of knowing: Natural history of a globally distributed team. *Journal of Organizational Behavior, 25*, 547–587. doi:10.1002/job.259

Barsade, S. G., & Gibson, D. E. (2012). Group affect its influence on individual and group outcomes. *Current Directions in Psychological Science, 21*(2), 119–123.

Beechler, S., & Woodward, I. C. (2009). The global "war for talent." *Journal of International Management, 15*(3), 273–285.

Berg, R. W. (2012). The anonymity factor in making multicultural teams work: Virtual and real teams. *Business Communication Quarterly, 75*(4), 404–424.

Brake, T. (2006). Leading global virtual team. *Industrial and Commercial Training, 38*(3), 116–121. doi:10.1108/00197850610659364

Briscoe, R. D., Schuler, S. R., & Claus, L. (2009). *International human resource management: Policies and practices for multinational enterprises* (5th ed.). New York, NY: Routledge.

Brownell, J., & Goldsmith, M. (2006). Commentary on "meeting the competency needs of global leaders: A partnership approach": An executive coach's perspective. *Human Resource Management, 45,* 309–336. doi:10.1002/hrm.20115

Cascio, W. F., & Shurygailo, S. (2003). E-leadership and virtual teams. *Organizational Dynamics, 31*(4), 362–376. doi:10.1016/s0090-2616(02)00130-4

Chang, H. H., Chuang, S. S., & Chao, S. H. (2011). Determinants of cultural adaptation, communication quality, and trust in virtual teams' performance. *Total Quality Management, 22*(3), 305–329.

Chen, G., Kirkman, B. L., Kim, K. H., Farh, C. I. C., & Tangirala, S. (2010). When does cross-cultural motivation enhance expatriate effectiveness? A multi-level investigation of the moderating roles of subsidiary support and cultural distance. *Academy of Management Journal, 53,* 1110–1130. doi:10.5465/AMJ.2010.54533217

Chiu, Y., & Staples, D. S. (2013). Reducing faultlines in geographically dispersed teams: Self-disclosure and task elaboration. *Small Group Research, 44*(5), 498–531. doi:10.1177/1046496413489735

Cohen, S. G., & Gibson, C. B. (2003). In the beginning: Introduction and framework. In C. B. Gibson & S. G. Cohen (Eds.), *Virtual teams that work: Creating conditions for virtual team effectiveness* (pp. 1–13). San Francisco, CA: Jossey-Bass.

Collings, D. G., & Mellahi, K. (2009). Strategic talent management: A review and research agenda. *Human Resource Management Review, 19*(4), 304–313.

Collings, D. G., Scullion, H., & Dowling, P. J. (2009). Global staffing: a review and thematic research agenda. *The International Journal of Human Resource Management, 20*(6), 1253–1272.

Connaughton, S. L., & Daly, J. A. (2004). Identification with leader: A comparison of perceptions of identification among geographically dispersed and co-located teams. *Corporate Communications: An International Journal, 9*(2), 89–103.

Cordery, J., Soo, C., Kirkman, B., Rosen, B., & Mathieu, J. (2009). Leading parallel global virtual team: Lessons from Alcoa. *Organizational Dynamics, 38*(3), 204–216.

Cramton, C. D. (2001). The mutual knowledge problem and its consequences for dispersed collaboration. *Organization Science, 12*(3), 346–371.

Crisp, C. B., & Jarvenpaa, S. L. (2013). Swift trust in global virtual team: Trusting beliefs and normative actions. *Journal of Personnel Psychology, 12*(1), 45.

Crossman, J., & Bordia, S. (2011). Friendship and relationships in virtual and intercultural learning: Internationalizing the business curriculum. *Australian Journal of Adult Learning, 51*(2), 329–354.

Daniel, S., Agarwal, R., & Stewart, K. J. (2013). The effects of diversity in global, distributed collectives: A study of open source project success. *Information Systems Research, 24*(2), 312–333. doi:10.1287/isre.1120.0435

Davis, D. D., & Bryant, J. L. (2003). Influence at a distance: Leadership in global virtual team. *Advances in Global Leadership, 3*, 303–340. doi:10.1016/s1535-1203(02)03015-0

DeChurch, L. A., & Mesmer-Magnus, J. R. (2010). The cognitive underpinnings of effective teamwork: A meta-analysis. *Journal of Applied Psychology, 95*(1), 32.

Dekker, D. M., Rutte, C. G., & Van den Berg, P. T. (2008). Cultural differences in the perception of critical interaction behaviors in global virtual team. *International Journal of Intercultural Relations, 32*(5), 441–452. doi:10.1016/j.ijintrel.2008.06.003

Dreo, H., Kunkel, P., & Mitchell, T. (2002). *Virtual teams guidebook for managers.* Milwaukee, WI: ASQ Quality Press.

Edmondson, A. (1999). Psychological safety and learning behavior in work teams. *Administrative Science Quarterly, 44*(2), 350–383.

Edmondson, A. C., Bohmer, R. M., & Pisano, G. P. (2001). Disrupted routines: Team learning and new technology implementation in hospitals. *Administrative Science Quarterly, 46*(4), 685–716.

Fain, N., & Kline, M. (2013). The dynamics of multicultural NPD teams in virtual environments. *International Journal of Technology and Design Education, 23*(2), 273–288.

Gatlin-Watts, R., Carson, M., Horton, J., Maxwell, L., & Maltby, N. (2007). A guide to global virtual teaming. *Team Performance Management, 13*(1/2), 47–52. doi:10.1108/13527590710736725

Gareis, E. (2006). Virtual teams: A comparison of online communication channels. *The Journal of Language for International Business, 17*(2), 6–21.

Gavidia, J. V., Mogollon, R. H., & Baena, C. (2004). Using international virtual teams in the business classroom. *Journal of Teaching in International Business, 16*(2), 51–74.

Germain, M. L. (2011). Developing trust in virtual teams. *Performance Improvement Quarterly, 24*(3), 29–54. doi:10.1002/piq.20119.

Gibson, C. B., & Cohen, S. G. (Eds.). (2003). *Virtual teams that work: Creating conditions for virtual team effectiveness.* Hoboken, NJ: John Wiley & Sons.

Gibson, C. B., & Gibbs, J. L. (2006). Unpacking the concept of virtuality: The effects of geographic dispersion, electronic dependence, dynamic structure, and national diversity on team innovation. *Administrative Science Quarterly, 51*(3), 451–495.

Glikson, E., & Erez, M. (2013). Emotion display norms in virtual teams. *Journal of Personnel Psychology, 12*(1), 22–32. doi:10.1027/1866-5888/a000078

Groeschl, S., & Doherty, L. (2000). Conceptualizing culture. *Cross Cultural Management, 7*(4), 12–17. doi:10.1108/13527600010797138

Gully, S. M., Devine, D. J., & Whitney, D. J. (2012). A meta–analysis of cohesion and performance effects of level of analysis and task interdependence. *Small Group Research, 43*(6), 702–725.

Gully, S. M., Incalcaterra, K. A., Joshi, A., & Beaubien, J. M. (2002). A meta-analysis of team-efficacy, potency, and performance: Interdependence and level of analysis as moderators of observed relationships. *Journal of Applied Psychology, 87*(5), 819.

Hardin, A. M., Fuller, M. A., & Davison, R. M. (2007). I know I can, but can we? Culture and efficacy beliefs in global virtual team. *Small Group Research, 38*(1), 130–155.

Hertel, G., Geiser, S., & Konradt, U. (2005). Managing virtual teams: A review of current empirical research. *Human Resource Management Review, 15*, 69–95. doi:10.1016/j.hrmr.2005.01.002

Hoftede, G., Hofstede, G. J., & Minkov, M. (2010). *Cultures and organizations: Software of the mind: Intercultural cooperation and its importance for survival.* New York, NY: McGraw-Hill.

Holtbrügge, D., & Schillo, K. (2011). Virtual delegation across borders: A knowledge-based perspective. *European Management Journal, 29*(1), 1–10. doi:10.1016/j.emj.2010.08.002

Jarvenpaa, S. L., & Keating, E. (2011). Hallowed grounds: The role of cultural values, practices, and institutions in TMS in an offshore complex engineering services project. *IEEE Transactions on Engineering Management, 58*(4), 786–798. doi:10.1109/TEM.2010.2091133

Jarvenpaa, S. L., Knoll, K., & Leidner, D. E. (1997). Is anybody out there? Antecedents of trust in global virtual team. *Journal of Management Information Systems, 14*(4), 29–64.

Jarvenpaa, S. L., & Leidner, D. E. (1998). Communication and trust in global virtual team. *Journal of Computer-Mediated Communication, 3*(4). doi:10.1111/j.1083-6101.1998.tb00080.x

Jarvenpaa, S. L., & Leidner, D. E. (1999). Communication and trust in GVTs. *Organization Science, 10*(6), 791–815.

Johansson, C., Dittrich, Y., & Juustila, A. (1999). Software engineering across boundaries: Student project in distributed collaboration. *IEEE Transactions on Professional Communication, 42*(4), 286–296.

Kahai, S. S., Sosik, J. J., & Avolio, B. J. (2003). Effects of leadership style, anonymity, and rewards on creativity-relevant processes and outcomes in an electronic meeting system context. *The Leadership Quarterly, 14*(4/5), 499–524. doi:10.1016/s1048-9843(03)00049-3

Kanawattanachai, P., & Yoo, Y. (2002). Dynamic nature of trust in virtual teams. *The Journal of Strategic Information Systems, 11*(3), 187–213.

Kanawattanachai, P., & Yoo, Y. (2007). The impact of knowledge coordination on virtual team performance over time. *MIS Quarterly, 31*, 783–808.

Kankanhalli, A., Tan, B. C., & Wei, K. K. (2007). Conflict and performance in global virtual team. *Journal of Management Information Systems, 23*, 237–274. doi:10.2753/MIS0742-1222230309

Kasper-Fuehrera, E. C., & Ashkanasy, N. M. (2001). Communicating trustworthiness and building trust in interorganizational virtual organizations. *Journal of Management, 27*(3), 235–254.

Kayworth, T., & Leidner, D. (2000). The global virtual manager: A prescription for success. *European Management Journal, 18*(2), 183–194. doi:10.1016/s0263-2373(99)00090-0

Kayworth, T. R., & Leidner, D. E. (2002). Leadership effectiveness in global virtual team. *Journal of Management Information Systems, 18*(3), 7–40.

Kirkman, B. L., & Mathieu, J. E. (2005). The dimensions and antecedents of team virtuality. *Journal of Management, 31*, 700–718. doi:10.1177/0149206305279113

Kirkman, B. L., Rosen, B., Gibson, C. B., Tesluk, P. E., & McPherson, S. O. (2002). Five challenges to virtual team success: Lessons from Sabre, Inc. *The Academy of Management Executive, 16*, 67–79. doi:10.5465/AME.2002.8540322

Klitmøller, A., & Lauring, J. (2013). When global virtual team share knowledge: Media richness, cultural difference and language commonality. *Journal of World Business, 48*, 398–406. doi:10.1016/j.jwb.2012.07.023

Kozlowski, S. W., & Ilgen, D. R. (2006). Enhancing the effectiveness of work groups and teams. *Psychological science in the public interest, 7*(3), 77–124.

Krumm, S., Terwiel, K., & Hertel, G. (2013). Challenges in norm formation and adherence: The knowledge, skills, and ability requirements of virtual and traditional cross-cultural teams. *Journal of Personnel Psychology, 12*(1), 33–44. doi:10.1027/1866-5888/a000077

Lurey, J. S., & Raisinghani, M. S. (2001). An empirical study of best practices in virtual teams. *Information & Management, 38*(8), 523–544.

Malhotra, A., Majchrzak, A., & Rosen, B. (2007). Leading virtual teams. *Academy of Management Perspectives, 21*(1), 60–70. doi:10.5465/amp.2007.24286164

Maloney, M. M., & Zellmer-Bruhn, M. E. (2006). Building bridges, windows and cultures: Mediating mechanisms between team heterogeneity and performance in global teams. *Management International Review, 46*, 697–720. doi:10.1007/s11575-006-0123-5

Martins, L. L., Gilson, L. L., & Maynard, M. T. (2004). Virtual teams: What do we know and where do we go from here? *Journal of Management, 30*, 805–835. doi:10.1016/j.jm.2004.05.002

Massey, A. P., Montoya-Weiss, M. M., & Hung, Y. (2003). Because time matters: Temporal coordination in global virtual project teams. *Journal of Management Information Systems, 19*(4), 129–155.

Maznevski, M. L., & Chudoba, K. M. (2000). Bridging space over time: Global virtual team dynamics and effectiveness. *Organization Science, 11*, 473–492. doi:10.1287/orsc.11.5.473.15200

McDonough, E. F., Kahnb, K. B., & Barczaka, G. (2001). An investigation of the use of global, virtual, and colocated new product development teams. *Journal of Product Innovation Management, 18*(2), 110–120.

Mockaitis, A. I., Rose, E. L., & Zettinig, P. (2012). The power of individual cultural values in global virtual team. *International Journal of Cross Cultural Management, 12*(2), 193–210. doi:10.1177/1470595812439868

Monalisa, M., Daim, T., Mirani, F., Dash, P., Khamis, R., & Bhusari, V. (2008). Managing global design teams. *Research Technology Management, 51*(4), 48–59.

Montoya-Weiss, M. M., Massey, A. P., & Song, M. (2001). Getting it together: Temporal coordination and conflict management in global virtual team. *Academy of Management Journal, 44*, 1251–1262. doi10.2307/3069399

Mortensen, M., & Hinds, P. J. (2001). Conflict and shared identity in geographically distributed teams. *International Journal of Conflict Management, 12*, 212–238. doi:10.1108/eb022856

Mukherjee, D., Lahiri, S., Mukherjee, D., & Billing, T. K. (2012). Leading virtual teams: How do social, cognitive, and behavioral capabilities matter? *Management Decision, 50*(2), 273–290. doi:10.1108/00251741211203560

Newell, S., David, G., & Chand, D. (2007). An analysis of trust among globally distributed work teams in an organizational setting. *Knowledge & Process Management, 14*(3), 158–168. doi:10.1002/kpm.284

Nonaka, I., & Takeuchi, H. (1995). *The knowledge creation company: how Japanese companies create the dynamics of innovation.* New York, NY: Oxford University Press.

Ocker, R. J., Huang, H., Benbunan-Fich, R., & Hiltz, S. R. (2011). Leadership dynamics in partially distributed teams: An exploratory study of the effects of configuration and distance. *Group Decision and Negotiation, 20*(3), 273–292. doi: 10.1007/s10726-009-9180-z

Oertig, M., & Buergi, T. (2006). The challenges of managing cross-cultural virtual project teams. *Team Performance Management, 12*(1), 23–30.

Panteli, N., & Davison, R. M. (2005). The role of subgroups in the communication patterns of global virtual team. *IEEE Transactions on Professional Communication, 48*(2), 191–200.

Panteli, N., & Tucker, R. (2009). Power and trust in global virtual team. *Communications of the ACM, 52*(12), 113–115.

Paul, S., Samarah, I. M., Seetharaman, P., & Mykytyn, P. P., Jr. (2004). An empirical investigation of collaborative conflict management style in group support system-based GVTs. *Journal of Management Information Systems, 21*, 185–222.

Pauleen, D. J. (2003a). Leadership in a global virtual team: An action learning approach. *Leadership & Organization Development Journal, 24*(3), 153–162.

Pauleen, D. J. (2003b). Lessons learned crossing boundaries in an ICT-supported distributed team. *Journal of Global Information Management, 11*(4), 1–19.

Pauleen, D. (Ed.). (2004). *Virtual teams: Projects, protocols and processes.* London, England: Idea Group.

Peters, L., & Karren, R. J. (2009). An examination of the roles of trust and functional diversity on virtual team performance ratings. *Group & Organization Management, 34*(4), 479–504. doi: 10.1177/1059601107312170

Pinjani, P., & Palvia, P. (2013). Trust and knowledge sharing in diverse global virtual team. *Information & Management, 50*(4), 144–153. doi:10.1016/j.im.2012.10.002

Piri, A., & Niinimaki, T. (2011, August). Does distribution make any difference? Quantitative comparison of collocated and globally distributed projects. In *Global software engineering workshop (ICGSEW), 2011* (pp. 24–30). Sixth IEEE International Conference, Helsinki, Finland. doi:10.1109/ICGSE-W.2011.23

Polzer, J. T., Crisp, C. B., Jarvenpaa, S. L., & Kim, J. W. (2006). Extending the faultline model to geographically dispersed teams: How co-located subgroups can impair group functioning. *Academy of Management Journal, 49*, 679–692. doi:10.5465/AMJ.2006.22083024

Powell, A., Piccoli, G., & Ives, B. (2004). Virtual teams: A review of current literature and directions for future research. *ACM Sigmis Database, 35*(1), 6–36.

Robert, L. P., Denis, A. R., & Hung, Y. T. C. (2009). Individual swift trust and knowledge-based trust in face-to-face and virtual team members. *Journal of Management Information Systems, 26*(2), 241–279.

Robey, D., Khoo, H. M., & Powers, C. (2000). Situated learning in cross-functional virtual teams. *Technical Communication, 47*(1), 51–66.

Rondinelli, D. A., & Heffron, J. M. (2009). *Leadership for development: What globalization demands of leaders fighting for change.* Sterling, VA: Kumarian Press.

Rosen, B., Furst, S., & Blackburn, R. (2006). Training for virtual teams: An investigation of current practices and future needs. *Human Resource Management, 45*(2), 229–247. doi:10.1002/hrm.20106

Salas, E., & Cannon-Bowers, J. A. (2001). The science of training: A decade of progress. *Annual Review of Psychology, 52*(1), 471–499.

Shachaf, P. (2005). Bridging cultural diversity through E-mail. *Journal of Global Information Technology Management, 8*(2), 46–60.

Shachaf, P. (2008). Cultural diversity and information and communication technology impacts on global virtual team: An exploratory study. *Information & Management, 45*(2), 131–142.

Shuffler, M. L., DiazGranados, D., & Salas, E. (2011). There's a science for the team development interventions in organizations. *Current Directions in Psychological Science, 20*(6), 365–372.

Sivunen, A. (2006). Strengthening identification with the team in virtual teams: The leaders' perspective. *Group Decision & Negotiation, 15*(4), 345–366. doi:10.1007/s10726-006-9046-6

Snow, C. C., Snell, S. A., Davison, S. C., & Hambrick, D. C. (1996). Use transnational teams to globalize your company. *Organizational Dynamics, 24*(4), 50–67.

Spencer, L. M., & Spencer, S. M. (1993). *Competency at work.* New York, NY: Wiley.

Staples, D. S., & Zhao, L. (2006). The effects of cultural diversity in virtual teams versus face-to-face teams. *Group Decision and Negotiation, 15,* 389–406. doi:10.1007/s10726-006-9042-x

Suchan, J., & Hayzak, G. (2001). The communication characteristics of virtual teams: A case study. *IEEE Transactions on Professional Communication, 44*(3), 174–186.

Umans, T. (2008). Ethnic identity, power, and communication in top management teams. *Baltic Journal of Management, 3*(2), 159–173. doi:10.1108/17465260810875497

Van Ryssen, S., & Godar, S. H. (2000). Going international without going international: Multinational virtual teams. *Journal of International Management, 6*(1), 49–60.

Vignovic, J. A., & Thompson, L. F. (2010). Computer-mediated cross-cultural collaboration: Attributing communication errors to the person versus the situation. *Journal of Applied Psychology, 95,* 265–276. doi:10.1037/a0018628

Vogel, D. R., Van Genuchten, M., Lou, D., Verveen, S., Van Eekout, M., & Adams, A. (2001). Exploratory research on the role of national and professional cultures in a distributed learning project. *IEEE Transactions on Professional Communication, 44*(2), 114–125.

Workman, M. (2007). The effects from technology-mediated interaction and openness in virtual team performance measures. *Behaviour & Information Technology, 26*(5), 355–365. doi:10.1080/01449290500402809

Yukl, G., Gordon, A., & Taber, T. (2002). A hierarchical taxonomy of leadership behavior: Integrating a half century of behavior research. *Journal of Leadership & Organizational Studies, 9*, 15–32. doi:10.1177/107179190200900102

Zaccaro, S. J., Rittman, A. L., & Marks, M. A. (2001). Team leadership. *The Leadership Quarterly, 12*(4), 451–483.

Zhouying, J. (2005). Globalization, technological competitiveness and the 'catch-up' challenge for developing countries: Some lessons of experience. *International Journal of Technology Management and Sustainable Development, 4*, 35–46.

Zigurs, I. (2003). Leadership in virtual teams. *Organizational Dynamics, 31*(4), 339–351. doi:10.1016/s0090-2616(02)00132-8

CHAPTER 8

TALENT DEVELOPMENT AND THE PERSISTENCE OF WORKING POOR FAMILIES

Richard Torraco

In this chapter, I address the persistence of working poor families and the causes and consequences of this problem. A working poor family is one in which at least one adult family member works full time the full year. Yet despite the wages earned, mostly from low-wage work, the family remains in poverty and is unable to attain basic financial security. This chapter will examine this issue in the United States and, when appropriate, discusses relevant aspects of this problem in the United Kingdom. Comparisons are also drawn across other developed nations to show the severity and prevalence of the problem.

The persistence of working poor families has three major causes: educational barriers faced by the working poor, recent changes in the job and labor market, and rising economic inequality. Inadequate education means that one is unlikely to get a job that pays family-supporting wages and the risk of drifting into the ranks of the working poor (Shipley, 2004). Changes in the job and labor market have expanded low-paying jobs and reduced incomes for a growing number of workers, contributing to the rise in poverty (Kalleberg, 2011). A third contributor to the persistence of working

Talent Development and the Global Economy:
Perspectives from Special Interest Groups, pp. 127–144
Copyright © 2017 by Information Age Publishing

poor families has been the dramatic growth in economic inequality in the United States and in other nations during the last three decades. Today the wealthiest 1% of the U.S. population get almost 25% of the nation's income (Stiglitz, 2012), and the richest 3% own 54.4% of the wealth in the United States (Federal Reserve Board, 2014). Rising income inequality is an international phenomenon with the United States and the United Kingdom leading the way (Wilkinson & Pickett, 2010). It has resulted in a greater concentration of wealth in the richest households, a diminished share of income for the poor, and the persistence of working poor families (Stiglitz, 2012).

I begin with a review of working poor families and low-wage work. Then, each of the three causes of the problem will be examined. Next, I explore the detrimental social and economic consequences of the persistence of working poor families. Finally, I discuss the implications of these developments for education and talent development.

WORKING POOR FAMILIES

A working poor family is defined by two characteristics: (a) the degree to which one or more members of the family participate in the labor market as wage earners, and (b) the annual combined income earned by all family members. A family is a married couple or single parent family with at least one co-resident child younger than 18 years old. A family is defined as working if all family members ages 15 and older either have a combined work effort of 39 weeks or more in the prior 12 months, or all family members ages 15 and older have a combined work effort of 26 to 39 weeks in the prior 12 months, and one currently unemployed parent has looked for work in the prior 4 weeks. A low-income family is defined as a family with an income below 200% of the poverty level, or double the threshold for poverty as defined by U.S. Census Bureau despite at least one family member working full time the full year (DeNavas-Walt, Proctor & Smith, 2013). Double the poverty threshold is used as a proxy for economic "self-sufficiency," the income a family requires to meet basic needs, including housing, food, clothing, health care, transportation, and childcare. In 2015, the poverty threshold for the United States averaged $24,250 for a family of four and thus the low-income threshold for a family of four averaged $48,500 (U.S. Department of Health and Human Services, 2015).

Poverty in the United States remains high at 15.1% with 46.5 million people living in poverty conditions. One-third of these people in severe poverty are faced with raising a child on less than $7,600 a year (Urban Institute, 2015). Children have the highest poverty rate among any age group. More than one in five children (21.8%) grows up in poverty. The poverty rate for individuals in unmarried female-headed families is 30.9%, compared with 9.7% for individuals in other types of families (United States Census Bureau, 2014).

Working Poor Families: Working Hard, But Falling Behind

What is low-wage work and what types of jobs do low-wage workers hold? They work long hours in retail jobs, care for children and the aged, work as cooks and waiters/waitresses, clean hotel rooms and offices, and do agricultural and other seasonal or temporary work. Oxfam America's study of low-wage workers in the United States found that low-wage workers are disproportionately women. The authors observed that:

> Work that pays low wages often falls into the realm of what has traditionally been considered women's work: domestic care (children and the elderly), health care, food service work, and cleaning. Because these jobs disproportionately employ women, the female workforce is challenged on several fronts: low wages, inadequate benefits to deal with family challenges, and the balance of home and work. Although women now make up close to half of the national workforce in the U.S., they substantially outnumber men in low-wage jobs. Women make up 60 % of the lower paying workforce. Almost 30% of the female workforce is low wage, in contrast to less than 20% of the male workforce. (Oxfam America, 2013, p. 7)

The study revealed that low-wage workers lead a precarious financial existence in which any setback may mean the difference between barely getting by and sliding further into poverty. Reflecting their seemingly endless financial concerns, most low-wage workers barely get by month to month, are burdened by worries about meeting their families' basic needs, and often rely on payday loans or loans from friends or family, government assistance, and credit card debt in their efforts to make ends meet. A substantial proportion of low-wage workers (79%) reported that they do not have enough savings available to provide for their family's basic needs for 3 months, a common measure of basic financial security (Oxfam America, 2013).

What do low-wage workers with families experience in their struggle to attain economic self-sufficiency? What is it like to work hard while losing ground financially? What happens to families who do not make living wages and are forced to make difficult choices between eating nutritious food, meeting health care needs, paying bills, and saving for emergencies?

Henry and Fredericksen (2013) explored some of the difficult choices facing working families who struggle to earn a living wage. They examined the living wage in six states by calculating the costs of basic needs such as housing, food, utilities, transportation, health care, and childcare for certain household sizes. Then they compared living wages with the percentage of job openings in the six states that paid less than a living wage to illustrate the *job gap*, the proportion of people who are forced to work in jobs that pay below a living wage because too few better paying jobs are available, and who are falling behind despite working full time. Although jobs that pay at least a living wage were available in the six states examined, there were between 20 and 39 job seekers for each job opening depending on the state. On the other hand, Henry and Fredericksen (2013) found an abundance of low-paying jobs; 80% of the jobs available paid less than a living wage for a single adult with two children. Low-wage work will be examined further in the section on the changing job market later in the chapter.

Now I turn to the causes of the persistence of working poor families. Inadequate education is a major factor contributing to the persistence of working poor families in the United States. Adults who are not prepared with the levels of knowledge and skills they need to get—and keep—good jobs are unable to earn family-supporting incomes and reluctantly drift into the ranks of the working poor (Shipley, 2004). Next, I will examine the relationships among education, socioeconomic status, and working poverty.

Educational Barriers and the Working Poor

Among the characteristics that contribute most to the vulnerability of the working poor and threaten their economic self-sufficiency is the lack of education, which could help get a job that pays family-supporting wages. Although the number of adults with an inadequate education who live on the threshold of poverty is unknown, many have deficiencies in basic skills (i.e., reading, writing, and/or mathematics) that are serious enough to hinder their participation in postsecondary education and in the modern workplace. Since basic skills form the foundation for the development of other knowledge and skills, deficiencies in these areas are obstacles to further education and prevent many adults from participating productively in the workplace.

The relationship between being deficient in basic skills and having a low income is important for understanding the characteristics of working poor families and their prospects for the future. Human capital liabilities (low education levels and limited work experience) and personal liabilities (poor physical and mental health) are associated with lower employment levels (Zedlewski, Holcomb, & Loprest, 2007). Low employment levels hinder the capacity to earn adequate income. Of course, there are many factors in addition to low levels of education that influence income level (i.e., language barriers, poor health, chemical dependency, learning disabilities, and criminal records). The unfortunate reality is that many adults in working poor families have basic skills that are generally considered insufficient for the modern workplace and consequently have low incomes. Moreover,

> Their low-income status feeds a vicious cycle in which the unavailability of financial resources for education restricts their ability to acquire additional skills needed for today's workplace, further hindering job advancement and their ability to move out of working poverty. (Torraco & Dirkx, 2009, p 4)

Without making claims about causal attribution, low-income levels, low job skills, and low educational achievement seem to go together.

The Changing Job Market and the Working Poor

Recent changes in the job market have exacerbated the persistence of working poor families in the United States (Bernhardt, 2012). Expansion in certain types of jobs and a decline in others are part of normal labor market fluctuations. Today web designers outnumber back tellers, whereas 20 years ago the reverse was true. The composition and availability of jobs are changing due to technological unemployment (e.g., machines replacing human workers; Brynjolfsson & McAfee, 2014), the increasing polarization of jobs into high-skill and low-skill occupations (Autor, 2010), and the rise in precarious employment. Proportionately more jobs are then what Kalleberg (2011) called precarious: those that are temporary, part-time, or seasonal. Expansion of these low paying jobs has meant stagnating incomes for the growing number of part-time and contingent workers and contributes to the rise in poverty. At the same time, jobs are polarized into high-skill and low-skill occupations, with declining opportunities in middle-wage and middle-skill jobs (Autor, 2010).

Technological Unemployment

Jobs are being eliminated by advances in technology, a phenomenon referred to by some as technological unemployment (Brynjolfsson & McAfee, 2014). Bank tellers have been replaced by ATMs; electro-mechanical assemblers have been replaced by robotics; tollbooth operators have been replaced by prepaid scanning technology; transcriptionists have been replaced by automated dictation systems; travel agents have been replaced by online travel and reservation systems; sales personnel have been displaced by web-enabled sales and e-commerce; and touchscreen menus have been introduced for ordering food from one's table in restaurants. Although the media frequently tout the wonders of new labor-saving technology, the list of jobs eliminated by advances in technology gets longer.

As information and computer technology displace workers from jobs, new jobs are not spawned in the process to replace those that were lost. Fewer new jobs are emerging in which human workers have a comparative advantage over computer-mediated machines and technology (Brynjolfsson & McAfee, 2014). Job loss today occurs more often through layoffs that are permanent, with new jobs created in different industries and occupations than where the jobs were lost (Manyika et al., 2011).

Polarization of Job Opportunities

Jobs have been polarized into high-skill and low-skill occupations, with declining opportunities in middle-wage, middle-skill, white-collar and blue-collar jobs. Employment and earnings are rising in high-education professional, technical, and managerial occupations; and while earnings are stagnant in low-education food service, personal care, and protective service occupations, job opportunities in these areas have risen since the late 1980s (Autor, 2010). The decline in middle-skill occupations has occurred in blue-collar jobs in manufacturing, machine shops, printing, textiles, and other areas vulnerable to routinization by computer technology, which allow employers to substitute capital and equipment for labor in jobs such as secretaries and administrative assistants, accounting and auditing specialists, typists and transcribers, telephone operators, utility meter readers, and stock and inventory clerks (Kalleberg, 2011).

The two factors that contribute most to the polarization of jobs are the automation of routine work and the international integration of labor markets (Autor, 2010). According to Autor, Levy, and Murname (2003), "A task is 'routine' if it can be accomplished by machines following explicit programmed rules" (p. 1283). Tasks are considered routine if they are well defined and can be accomplished successfully by a computer program. These tasks are also susceptible to off-shoring to developing countries to save labor costs. The core responsibilities of jobs such as transcriptionists, utility meter readers, and electro-mechanical assemblers consist of routine tasks that generally follow well-defined procedures, which increasingly can be written into software and performed electronically or, alternatively, sent electronically overseas to be completed at a comparatively lower cost by low-skilled workers (Autor, 2010).

Declining Job Quality

Another challenge faced by workers is the shift away from full-time jobs to more part-time, contingent, and seasonal jobs—referred to as precarious employment (Kalleberg, 2011). In addition to being precarious, these jobs generally pay low wages, lack health insurance, and do not provide pension benefits (Kalleberg, 2011). In 2010, 20% of working adults aged 25 to 64 held jobs that paid wages less than what was needed to keep a family of four above the U.S. poverty level (Osterman & Schulman, 2011). The jobs of 14.3% of U.S. workers, or about one in seven, paid low wages, lacked health insurance, and did not provide pensions (Kalleberg, 2011). Reflecting the precarious position of those with part-time and contingent jobs, employers are less likely to offer benefits and more likely to pay low wages to workers in these jobs. Employers who create more part-time jobs know that they can avoid providing health care coverage since there are no penalties under the Affordable Care Act for not covering part-time employees (Henry & Fredericksen, 2013). Next I examine the relationship between socioeconomic status and working poverty.

Rising Economic Inequality and the Working Poor

Another key contributor to the persistence of working poor families has been the dramatic growth in economic inequality in the United States during the last three decades. Rising economic inequality is demonstrated by comparing the distribution of wealth among the U.S. population over time. Household wealth is the sum of all assets, such as property, car, investments, and other financial assets minus the sum of all debts and liabilities, such as mortgages, credit card debt, and loans (Fry & Taylor, 2013). While the wealthiest top 1% of the United States population now gets almost 25% of the nation's income, and the richest 3% own 54.4% of the wealth, the share of wealth owned by the bottom 90% of the population has declined since the mid-1980s to 23% in 2012 (Saez & Zucman, 2014). The poverty rate increased from 12.5% in 2007 to 15% in 2013 (Stanford Center on Poverty and Inequality, 2014). Rising income inequality has resulted in a greater concentration of wealth in the richest households, a diminished share of income for the poor, and the persistence of working poor families in the United States.

Growing economic inequality is not limited to the United States alone, it is a global phenomenon. The *Gini coefficient*, an international measure of income inequality, shows high income inequality in sub-Saharan Africa and South America and low-income inequality in Scandinavia and northern Europe (World Bank Group, 2016). Using international comparisons and historical analysis, Piketty (2014) demonstrated the growing concentration of wealth by elites in an increasing number of countries, and cited the deleterious consequences of trends in wealth distribution that can be traced to the 19th century. Today the richest 85 people in the world own more wealth than the bottom half of the entire global population (i.e., 3 billion people): The equation works out to: 85 > 3,000,000,000 (Oxfam International, 2014).

In summary, educational barriers, the changing job and labor market, and rising economic inequality contribute to the persistence of working poor families. These problems are difficult to address because their causes are complex and multidimensional. Figure 8.1 shows these three contributors to the persistence of working poor families.

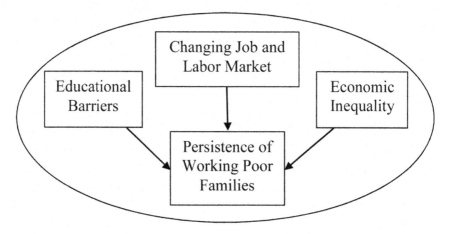

Figure 8.1.   Factors That Contribute to the Persistence of the Working Poor

THE CONSEQUENCES OF THE PERSISTENCE OF WORKING POOR FAMILIES

The growth and intractable nature of working poor families are themselves serious problems. In addition, however, there are detrimental social and economic consequences due to this problem. Next, I will examine the social and economic consequences of these developments on educational achievement, intergenerational social mobility, social relations, crime and imprisonment, health, and democracy.

Educational Achievement

The detrimental effects of the persistence of working poor families and growing economic inequality appear in the increasing disparity in educational achievement among students of wealthy and poor families in the United States and in other countries. Examining education for children in Britain, Benn and Millar (2006) concluded that one of the most serious problems was not with the British schools themselves, but the gap between the rich and poor and the substantial disparity in support that children received for education from their family and home environments. Comparing data from each state, Wilkinson and Pickett (2010) demonstrated that states in the United States with greater economic inequality had lower educational achievement. They showed a similar relationship on an international scale across 23 developed countries. Those with greater economic inequality had lower scores in math and literacy, led by the United States, Portugal, and the United Kingdom, while countries with more equitable distributions of income such as Japan and the Scandinavian countries showed higher scores.

Intergenerational Social Mobility

The relationship between income inequality and intergenerational social mobility in several countries has been plotted in what is known as the *Great Gatsby Curve*. The curve shows intergenerational income elasticity, which is the likelihood that someone will inherit their parents' relative position of income level. The curve was introduced in a speech by the chairman of the Council of Economic Advisers, Alan Krueger (2012), using data later published by labor economist Miles Corak (2013). Countries with low levels of inequality such as Denmark, Norway, and Finland had the greatest intergenerational mobility; while the two countries with high levels of income inequality, the United States and the United Kingdom, had the lowest mobility. A chart with the Great Gatsby Curve is shown in Figure 8.2.

The Great Gatsby Curve shows that the United States has the highest levels of income inequality and social immobility among the developed nations shown. This means that a parent's income is a good predictor of a child's subsequent income. It also means that parental income matters more for children's success in the United States than in other economically developed countries. Because income inequality in the United States is increasing, the gap between those with advantages and disadvantages due to the transfer of parental income to their children is expected to grow by 25% for the next generation (Wilkinson & Pickett, 2010). These figures make it difficult to not be concerned that rising inequality is jeopardizing the American tradition of equality of opportunity.

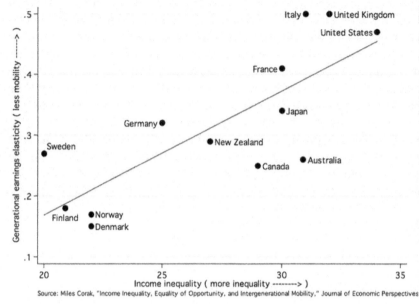

Source: Miles Corak, "Income Inequality, Equality of Opportunity, and Intergenerational Mobility," Journal of Economic Perspectives

Source: Corak (2013). Reprinted with permission.

Figure 8.2.   The Great Gatsby curve.

Social Relations

The persistence of poverty and high income inequality is associated with lower levels of trust among people, leading to the deterioration of social relations in less equal societies. Using a random sample of the populations of 23 countries, researchers found that the percentage of people agreeing that "most people can be trusted" is higher in more equal countries (Uslaner, 2002). Illustrating the differences among the countries sampled, Norway, which is a country with low income inequality and high levels of trust, is characterized by the public availability of food and blankets for those in need, and neighborhoods where people leave their doors unlocked. Whereas these conditions are hard to imagine in the United States.

Crime and Imprisonment

Crime and imprisonment are problems that are deeply rooted in the culture and norms of societies. People with less education and lower incomes are more likely to be imprisoned than those higher on the social scale; a reflection of the relationship between income inequality and imprisonment (Western & Pettit, 2010). In blunt fashion, Wilkinson and Pickett (2010) summarized the difference in attitudes toward punishment versus rehabilitation and reform:

> In societies with greater inequality, where the social distances between people are greater, where attitudes of "us and them" are more entrenched, and where lack of trust and fear of crime are rife, public and policy makers alike are more willing to imprison people and adopt punitive attitudes toward the "criminal elements" of society. (p. 155)

Increasing economic inequality also is leading to higher rates of imprisonment for the economically and educationally disadvantaged (Western, Kleykamp, & Rosenfeld, 2004).

Health and Obesity

World Health Organization data on poverty, income inequality, and health outcomes show that more equal societies tend to be healthier (Demyttenaere, 2004). How evenly wealth is distributed seems more important than the overall wealth of a society in determining its health status and mortality. Greater income inequality is associated with lower life expectancy, higher rates of infant mortality, shorter height, poor self-reported health, low birth weight, AIDS, and depression (Demyttenaere, 2004). In addition, obesity rates among adults and children are higher in more unequal countries. While stress, over eating, and lack of exercise contribute to the problem, obesity among the poor is strongly associated with their low-income status (Pickett, Kelly, Brunner, Lobstein, & Wilkinson, 2005).

Summarizing their analysis of the relationship between income inequality and several important social outcomes such as educational performance, health and life expectancy, crime and incarceration rates, teenage births, social mobility, and levels of trust and social cohesion, Wilkinson and Pickett (2010) concluded:

> If you want to know why one country does better or worse than another, the first thing to look at is the extent of inequality. There is not one policy for reducing inequality in health or the educational performance of school children, and another for raising national standards of performance. Reducing inequality is the best way of doing both. (pp. 29–30)

Public Disenfranchisement, Reduced Voting and Civic Participation

A foundation of democracy is the right and obligation of United States citizens to vote in elections and to participate in other civic responsibilities. One's willingness to vote is based, in part, on trust in the electoral process and the belief that one's vote matters (Burnham, 2010). However, rising economic inequality feeds public disenfranchisement as people with stagnant or declining incomes lose hope in the future. Economic inequality inevitably translates into political inequality. America's politics are increasingly better characterized, Stiglitz (2012) believes, as a system not of "one person, one vote" but of "one dollar, one vote" (p. 139). But the effects of public disillusionment and the erosion of trust are not limited to lower voter turnout and civic participation. Friedman (2005) argued that no matter how wealthy a society becomes, it is not immune from the erosion of its basic values when a majority of its citizens lose their sense of forward economic progress. Emphasizing the relationship between economic growth and the moral characteristics of society he stated, "Economic growth is not only an enabler of higher consumption, it is in many ways the wellspring from which democracy and civil society flow" (Friedman, 2005, p. 68).

In summary, rising economic inequality contributes to the persistence of working poor families. It also contributes to the wide range of deleterious social and economic consequences reviewed suggested earlier. The model of the factors that contribute to the persistence of the working poor (Figure 8.1) is amended here to show that these developments lead to serious social and economic consequences.

While it is difficult to deny that economic inequality is rising in the United States and in other countries, some deny its importance by citing widely discredited trickle-down economics that falsely implies that income inequality and more wealth for the rich benefits everybody and is necessary for economic growth (Krueger, 2012). Others deny its injustice by attributing dramatic wealth disparities to the mistaken belief that the ultrarich simply work more than the rest of us (Rector & Hederman, 2004). And then there are some who may see rising economic inequality as a problem, but envision its resolution by a "technological fix to inequality" that seems based on little more than wishful thinking (Cowen, 2014, p. 7).

What is the role of education in addressing the problems of poverty and economic inequality? How can education reduce the prevalence of working poor families? In response, some ask why should educational leaders be concerned about the persistence of working poor families? Instead, we should ask what are educational leaders doing to address this growing problem? Why are they not doing more? This problem is too important to

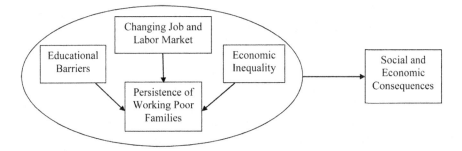

Figure 8.3.   Factors that contribute to the persistence of the working poor and its consequences.

be left to politics and policymakers alone. Next, I will address the implications of this problem for education and talent development.

IMPLICATIONS FOR EDUCATION AND TALENT DEVELOPMENT

Most working poor families are eager to achieve the means for economic self-sufficiency. They seek the education and skills they need to get a job that pays family-supporting wages. This is an education issue. Education has always been a way in which upward mobility can get started. During the latter half of the 20th century widespread educational opportunity eroded class barriers and was referred to as "the great equalizer" (DeParle, 2012, p. 14).

Greater Access to Postsecondary Education

Contrary to its egalitarian tradition, postsecondary education recently has become more expensive and exclusive (College Board, 2015). Greater access to postsecondary education is needed for all, not just the wealthy and privileged. The detrimental effects of college costs and growing economic inequality appear in the increasing disparity in educational achievement among students of wealthy and poor families. High student test scores and high family income both have positive correlations with the likelihood of college graduation (Belley & Lochner, 2007; Turner, 2004). But increasing economic inequality has widened the gap in family incomes and contributed to declining educational opportunity. Bailey and Dynarski (2011) demonstrated that high-income students with low test scores are more likely to graduate from college than low-income students with high test scores. Among the explanations for this disparity are more support and investment by wealthy parents in their children's learning and enrichment activities, such as music lessons, travel, and summer camps, and the multiple barriers to educational achievement faced by poor students. But "if only the prosperous become educated—and only the educated prosper —the schoolhouse risks becoming just another place where the fortunate preserve their edge" (DeParle, 2012, pp. 14–15). Greater access to postsecondary education is needed for all, including working poor families.

Greater Responsiveness to the Working Poor

Within postsecondary education, 2-year community colleges make the most effort to be responsive to the needs of the labor market and those who seek job training (Altstadt, 2011). America's community colleges traditionally have offered hope for those seeking re-entry into the education system.

Despite the tradition of open access, community colleges have struggled to accommodate more applicants, including the working poor. One reason is that preparation in basic skills and occupational training for the workforce that are needed by the working poor are often misperceived by traditional administrators and faculty as low-status activities that do not warrant consideration as a real college program (Grubb, 1999). Consequently these programs are often marginalized by low funding and inadequate staffing. Altering this perception requires cultural change that is at best gradual and complex, and requires a shift in values, attitudes, and incentives that often occur grudgingly in academic institutions where change is slow and incremental. As recommended in a guide to best practices, "Traditional academic views of workforce development activity must change if a community college is to embrace the mission of labor market responsiveness" (U.S. Department of Education, 2004, p. 23).

Greater pressure on community colleges for academic and fiscal accountability creates another barrier to their responsiveness to the working poor. Shrinking budgets have forced colleges to make painful choices to use scarce resources for degree programs rather than for remedial courses. Edgecombe, Cormier, Birckstaff, and Barragin (2013) found that community colleges, under greater pressure to graduate more students, are enacting reforms that undermine efforts to help underprepared students such as raising admission requirements that compromise open access. This shift adversely affects the millions of low-income and minority students who apply to community colleges every year, many of whom need remedial education first. But policymakers and reformers want to see a single figure: completions. How many students graduated? How many did not? These figures often do not account for students' personal and social development, and mean that second chance opportunities offered only by community colleges are further out of reach for working poor and minority students (Torraco & Hamilton, 2016). As characterized by a report in *The Chronicle of Higher Education*, "The community is being stripped out of community college" (Gonzalez, 2012, p. 7).

Mismatch in Workforce Supply and Demand

A final implication of the persistence of working poor families for education and talent development is its effect on the workforce and economic development. The educational requirements for jobs in the next decade are rising. By 2020, 65% of all jobs in the United States economy will require postsecondary education and training beyond high school (Carnevale, Smith & Strohl, 2013). However, the fastest growing racial/ethnic portion of the United States population, Hispanics, is the least educated and most likely to drop out of school (Kelly, 2005). These demographic changes in the supply of future workers can be compared with the demand for educated workers in the future labor force. While the educational preparation for jobs in the next decade is rising (Carnevale et al., 2013), the education and skills of those who will be in the workforce during this period are stagnant (Kelly 2005). This mismatch between the high skills of future jobs and the declining education levels of the workforce needs to be corrected to support a strong economy and opportunity for all (Kirsch, Braun, Yamamoto, & Sum, 2007).

REFERENCES

Altstadt, D. (2011). *Aligning community colleges to their local labor markets.* Boston, MA: Jobs for the Future.

Autor, D. H. (2010). *The polarization of job opportunities in the U.S. labor market: Implications for employment and earnings.* Washington, DC: Center for American Progress.

Autor, D. H., Levy, F. & Murname, R. J. (2003). The skill content of recent technological change: An empirical exploration. *The Quarterly Journal of Economics, 116*(4), 1279–1333.

Bailey, M. J., & Dynarski, S. M. (2011). Inequality in postsecondary education. In G. J. Duncan & R. J. Murname (Eds.), *Whither opportunity? Rising inequality, schools, and children's life chances.* New York, NY: Russell Sage Foundation.

Belley, P., & Lochner, L. (2007). The changing role of family income and ability in determining educational achievement. *Journal of Human Capital, 1*(1), 37–89.

Benn, M., & Millar, F. (2006). *A comprehensive future: Quality and equality for all our children*. London, England: Compass.

Bernhardt, A. (2012). *The low-wage recovery and growing inequality*. New York, NY: National Employment Law Project.

Brynjolfsson, E., & McAfee, A. (2014). *The second machine age: Work, progress, and prosperity in a time of brilliant technologies*. New York, NY: Norton.

Burnham, W. D. (2010). *Democracy in peril: The American turnout problem and the path to plutocracy*. Working Paper, No. 5. Hyde Park, NY: Roosevelt Institute.

Carnevale, A. P., Smith, N., & Strohl, J. (2013). *Recovery: Job growth and education requirements through 2020*. Washington, DC: Center on Education and the Workforce, Georgetown University.

College Board. (2015). *Tuition and fees and room and board over time*. Retrieved from http://trends.collegeboard.org/college-pricing/figures-tables/tuition-fees-room-board-time

Corak, M. (2013). Income inequality, equality of opportunity, and intergenerational mobility. *Journal of Economic Perspectives, 27* (3), 72–102.

Cowen, T. (2014, December 7). The technological fix to inequality. *The New York Times*, p. 7.

Demyttenaere, K. (2004). Prevalence, severity, and unmet needs for treatment of mental disorders in the World Health Organization world mental health surveys. *JAMA, 291*(21), 2581–2590.

DeNavas-Walt, C., Proctor, B. D., & Smith, J. C. (2013). *Income, poverty, and health insurance coverage in the United States: 2012*. Washington, DC: U.S. Census Bureau.

DeParle, J. (2012, December 23). For poor, leap to college often ends in a hard fall. *The New York Times*, pp. 10–15.

Edgecombe, N., Cormier, M. S., Bickerstaff, S., & Barragan, M. (2013). *Strengthening developmental education reforms: Evidence on implementation efforts from the scaling innovation project*. CCRC Working Paper No. 61. New York, NY: Community College Research Center, Teachers College, Columbia University.

Federal Reserve Board. (2014). Changes in U.S. family finances from 2010 to 2013: Evidence from the survey of consumer finances. *Federal Reserve Bulletin, 100*(4).

Friedman, B. M. (2005). *The moral consequences of economic growth*. New York, NY: Knopf.

Fry, R., & Taylor, P. (2013). *A rise in wealth for the wealthy: Declines for the lower 93%*. Washington, DC: Pew Research Center.

Gonzalez, J. (2012, April 22). Education for all? Two-year colleges struggle to preserve their mission: Two-year colleges fight to save access for all. *The Chronicle of Higher Education, 79*, 6–7.

Grubb, W. N. (1999). *Honored but invisible: An inside look at teaching in community colleges*. New York, NY: Routledge.

Henry, B., & Fredericksen, A. (2013). *Broken bootstraps: Falling behind on full-time work*. Seattle, WA: Alliance for a Just Society.

Kalleberg, A. L. (2011). *Good jobs, bad jobs: The rise of polarized and precarious employment systems in the United States, 1970 to 2000s*. New York, NY: Russell Sage Foundation.

Kelly, P. J. (2005). *As America becomes more diverse: The impact of state higher education inequality*. Boulder, CO: National Center for Higher Education Management Systems.

Kirsch, I., Braun, H., Yamamoto, K., & Sum, A. (2007). *America's perfect storm: Three forces changing our nation's future*. Princeton, NJ: Educational Testing Service.

Krueger, A. B. (2012, January 12). *The rise and consequences of inequality in the United States: Presentation for the Center for American Progress*. Washington, DC: Author.

Manyika, J., Lund, S., Auguste, B. Mendonca, L., Welsh, T. & Ramaswamy, S. (2011). *An economy that works: Job creation and America's future*. Retrieved from www.mckinsey.com.mgi

Osterman, P., & Schulman, B. (2011). *Good jobs America: How to make work better for everyone*. New York, NY: Russell Sage.

Oxfam America. (2013). *Hard work, hard lives: Survey exposes harsh reality faced by low-wage workers in the U.S.* Retrieved from http://www.oxfamamerica.org/files/hart-low-wage-workers-survey

Oxfam International. (2014). *Working for the few: Political capture and economic inequality*. Oxfam Briefing Paper No. 178. Oxford, England: Oxfam GB.

Pickett, K. E., Kelly, S., Brunner, E., Lobstein, T., & Wilkinson, R. G. (2005). Wider income gaps, wider waistbands? An ecological study of obesity and income inequality. *Journal of Epidemiology and Community Health, 59*(8), 670–674.

Piketty, T. (2014). *Capitalism in the 21st century*. Cambridge, MA: Harvard University Press.

Rector, R., & Hederman, R. (2004). *Two Americas: One rich, one poor? Understanding income inequality in the United States*. Washington, DC: The Heritage Foundation.

Saez, E., & Zucman, G. (2014). *Wealth inequality in the United States since 1913: Evidence from capitalized income tax data*. Working paper No. 20615. Cambridge, MA: National Bureau of Economic Research.

Shipley, D. K. (2004). *The working poor: Invisible in America*. New York, NY: Vintage Books.

Stanford Center on Poverty and Inequality. (2014). *The poverty and inequality report*. Stanford, CA: Author.

Stiglitz, J. E. (2012). *The price of inequality: How today's divided society endangers our future*. New York, NY: Norton.

Torraco, R. J., & Dirkx, J. M. (2009). Academically underprepared adults: An exploration into their diversity and educational needs. In T. Chermack (Ed.), *Academy of human resource development conference proceedings* (pp. 2–10). Bowling Green, OH: Academy of Human Resource Development.

Torraco, R. J., & Hamilton, D. W. (2016). Family incomes fall, while admission requirements rise: Implications for community colleges. *Community College Journal of Research and Practice, 40*(9), 797–801.

Turner, S. (2004). Going to college and finishing college: Explaining different educational outcomes. In C. Hoxby (Ed.), *College choices: The economics of where to go, when to go, and how to pay for it*. Chicago, IL: University of Chicago Press.

Urban Institute. (2015). *Understanding poverty: Advancing our understanding of effective anti-poverty policy*. Retrieved from http://www.urban.org/features/understanding-poverty

Uslaner, E. (2002). *The moral foundations of trust.* Cambridge, England: Cambridge University Press.

United States Census Bureau. (2014). *Income and poverty in the United States: 2013, current population reports.* Washington, DC: U.S. Department of Commerce, Economics and Statistics Administration.

United States Department of Education. (2004). *The 21st century community college: A strategic guide to maximizing labor market responsiveness: Promising practices and lessons from the field* (Vol. 2). Washington, DC: Office of Vocational and Adult Education.

United States Department of Health and Human Services. (2015). *Poverty guidelines for the 48 contiguous states and the District of Columbia.* Retrieved from https://aspe.hhs.gov/2015-poverty-guidelines

Western, B., Kleykamp, M., & Rosenfeld, J. (2004). *Economic inequality and the rise in U.S. imprisonment.* Princeton, NJ: Department of Sociology, Princeton University.

Western, B., & Pettit, B. (2010). Incarceration and social inequality. *Daedalus: Journal of the American Academy of Arts and Sciences, 48,* 8–19.

Wilkinson, R., & Pickett, K. (2010). *The spirit level: Why greater equality makes societies stronger.* New York, NY: Bloomsbury Press.

World Bank Group. (2016). *Gini index (World Bank estimate).* Washington, DC: The World Bank Group. Retrieved from http://data.worldbank.org/indicator/SI.POV.GINI/

Zedlewski, S. R., Holcomb, P., & Loprest, P. (2007). *Hard-to-employ parents: A review of their characteristics and the programs designed to serve their needs.* Washington, DC: The Urban Institute.

CHAPTER 9

TALENT DEVELOPMENT IN THE 21ST CENTURY AND SOCIAL MEDIA

Fatemeh Rezaei and Misha Chakraborty

Despite the increasingly significant role of technology and the popularity of social media among a new generation of employees, there are only a few studies related to the impact and benefits of utilizing social media as a human resource development (HRD) tool in organizations. There has been a major change in the number of organizations that consider using technology in their work process. This trend can be described

> as moving away from a limited view of technology as a physical artifact with its own independent realm of action, and moving toward a systems-centered view that allows greater understanding of complexity, professional life world, and application driven by an organization's vision for technology. (Benette, 2014, p. 263)

The technology oriented movement has affected human resource management and development fields (Bennett, 2009). Yoon and Lim (2010) believe that technologies and virtual human resource development (VHRD) force HRD practitioners to play the role of work solution partner rather than experts of learning in organizations. Short (2010), in his reflections on

Talent Development and the Global Economy:
Perspectives from Special Interest Groups, pp. 145–153
Copyright © 2017 by Information Age Publishing
All rights of reproduction in any form reserved.

VHRD from the perspective of a scholar-practitioner, mentioned that along with other factors that challenge the field of HRD such as speed of change and global organizations, technology is becoming more advanced and prevalent than ever, and the new generations of employees consider technology an integration tool for their work and life. In his opinion, there is a significant opportunity for HRD researchers and practitioners to build a foundational theory for HRD that explains the VHRD challenges, benefits, effectiveness, and contributions in the HRD field. One of these emerging areas is application of social media in talent development.

Social media paints the new communication landscape where people are more connected than ever, and at the same time they are more disconnected than ever (Cappelli, 2009). The ecology of social media is diverse, ranging from Hi5, Facebook, Twitter, to LinkedIn, which is focused toward building a professional network. Media sharing sites like YouTube, Flickr, Myspace, and so forth, are gaining increasing popularity. Various blog sites (e.g., weblogs, blogospheres) are very popular in depicting opinions, citing other resources, positing "status updates," etc. The phenomenal increase in social media networking is seen as "democratized" communication in the corporate sector (Kietzmann, Hermkens, McCarthy, & Silvestre, 2011). People are free to express their views from sellers' and buyers' perspectives. The open communication systems need planned strategies to ensure optimum use of social media usage from the organizations' sides.

The organizations can decide whether to ignore the tremendous power of communication happening through social media or create, share, and follow strategies to use for their own business benefits and talent management. The recent trends show the companies are paying attention to the use of social media as a business tool. For instance, *The New York Times Magazine* has a social media editor (Nolan, 2009).

BACKGROUND

Solmon (2010) and Neo (2010) explained through their research that there are different preferences of new Generation X and Y learners and workforces in using social network sites, flexible access to information, and self-directed learning environments. McWhorter (2010) referred to different types of technological methods and tools such as personal computers, Web 2.0, 3D virtual worlds, and virtual communities that allow human resource experts to develop and create effective HRD interventions in the new rapidly changing work environment.

Another example of social media is Facebook, which with 94% of Internet users is known as the first popular social media in the United States and the world (Statista, 2014). As of June 2014, Facebook had more than

1.32 billion global monthly active users. This statistic also shows a timeline with the worldwide number of active Facebook users from 2008 to 2014. As of the third quarter of 2014, Facebook had 1.35 billion monthly active users. In the third quarter of 2012, the number of active Facebook users had surpassed 1 billion. The number of Facebook active users in the United States as of April 2013 was 148.6 million. Active users are those who have logged in to Facebook during the last 30 days (Statista, 2014).

Although LinkedIn is not one of the most popular social media sites, exploring its features and effects on individuals' networks is important because it is one of the most-used and famous professional social media website. LinkedIn is a social networking site for professionals. With close to 300 million members worldwide, it is one of the most popular social networks in terms of active users in the professional world. During the third quarter of 2014, LinkedIn had 332 million members, up from 296 million members in the first quarter of that year. This statistic ranked countries worldwide by number of registered members of LinkedIn as of October 2014: the United States had 107 million users; the United Kingdom had more than 17 million registered users; and Canada had more than 10 million registered users. Overall, the professional social network had more than 80 million members in European countries. Garg and Telang (2012) brought statistics about the percentage of online job seekers who use LinkedIn and other popular job search platforms. The more popular job search boards (like monster.com or indeed.com) are visited by approximately 0.25% of Internet users, each person spending 4 minutes per day on average at these websites, while LinkedIn is consumed by 3.4% of daily Internet users, each user spending 7.4 minutes per day on average.

Reflecting on the statistics reports, it is conceivable to claim that social media can provide a room to make a balance between high-tech interventions and high-tough interactions among people (specifically employees in organizations), which according to Wang (2012) reaching that balance is one of the important challenges HRD practitioners confront.

ISSUES, CONTROVERSIES, AND PROBLEMS

The purpose of this chapter is to find out the relation between social media and talent development and also to present the recent trends in organizations related to use of social media in talent development.

Our thorough search generated a large volume of literature related to social media or talent management, in general, but a very small number of publications on talent development and social media. While many articles address social media and talent management separately, we found fewer than 10 articles that used the term social media in the context of talent management.

One of the strongest criticisms of using social media in the workplace is the negative perception of managers and even employees about it. They think that it wastes employees' time and an organizations' money. They believed that social media was created for personal use and employees use it for non-work-related purposes. In addition, inappropriate use of social media, personal use, misbehaviors like racist comments, or sharing inappropriate information are considered as challenges of implementing social media as a talent management tool within the whole organization. Moreover, HRD professionals should be sensitive to the privacy of information and make sure that those who are competitors of organization cannot track organizations data and decisions if the organization is using social media in order to share knowledge and ideas.

RESULTS

This section highlights some significant areas identified in present literature related to the use of social media in talent management. Social media creates the unique platform that enables users to create, disseminate, participate, and get involved in user-generated content (Kietzmann et al., 2011). Both nonprofit and for-profit organizations maintain various social network sites in their day-to-day business.

Boyd and Ellison (2008) tracked the evolution of social media and found out that about 12 years back social media started to get popular. In 1997, Six Degrees (SixDigrees.com, a social network site) allowed users to open an account, add friends and friend's friends. Sites like YouTube and various blogging sites are used in meetings or training sessions in companies to deliver content to the users.

Social networks such as Facebook, Twitter, LinkedIn, wikis, and social bookmarks are some of the most cited technologies or tools in Web 2.0 that have affected the HRD field in many ways, like knowledge sharing and training (Wang, 2012). Social media enhances human interactions in virtual environment among individuals who might be physically dispersed (Wang, 2012)

According to numerous researchers (e.g., Aral, Dellarocas, & Godees, 2013; Lin & Lazar, 2013; Mount & Martinez, 2014), social media has changed communication and knowledge sharing. Social media features along with their popularity, especially in the United States, allow users to participate more in discussions, engage in knowledge sharing, and be passionate about personal relationships along with vocational relationships. For example, Twitter, the second most popular social media in the world

(26% of Internet users in the United States), currently has 284 million monthly active users, and 500 million Tweets are sent per day (Kietzmann et al., 2011). Statistics show a forecast of the number of active Twitter users in the United States from 2012 to 2018. From all over the world, it was found that 50.9% of worldwide Twitter users were located in the United States. Lin and Lazar (2013) developed a visualization tool, Whisper, to show how, when, where, and what kinds of information has been spread through Twitter. They believed that tracing the tweets in a real time manner could help detect the opinion leader and identify the popularity of an idea.

Kietzmann et al. (2011) proposed the honeycomb structure of social media that consists of aspects like identity, conversation, sharing, presence, relationship, reputations, and groups. Besides common features of all social media, individual social media has been designed to fulfill some specific needs. For example, YouTube focuses on sharing videos, Twitter promotes short conversations, and Facebook helps users connection with their friends.

LinkedIn is a popular network site that enables users to build professional networks. The job seeker and candidate seekers have hugely benefited from using this channel to reach out to each other, post and see job advertisements, and expand their professional networks (Kaplan & Haenlein, 2010).

Aral et al., (2013) discussed the role of social media in making connections with remote talent and matching the job with the appropriate talent. They stated that one of the possible research frameworks within the area of social media would be exploring answers to questions like how organizations and firms would utilize social media's features to benefit their business; and how organizations and firms can choose from the different kinds of initiatives social platforms offer to maximize their effectiveness and make sure that they are aligned with an organization's strategies. They believed that although using social media-related interventions could be a powerful tool to develop knowledge sharing and employees' interaction, it can waste the financial and human resources of the organization if appropriate tools or features have not been chosen. They also noted that social media would manipulate decision-making process of employees and therefore cause production of higher quality decisions, because employees are encouraged to consider the other aspects of a subject through such huge opinions and ideas. In addition, application of social media in sharing knowledge and ideas, collaborative online training, and building social networks with a low-cost investment are the other benefits of using social media (Garg & Telang, 2012; Lin & Lazer, 2013; Roberts & Sambrook, 2013; Thomas & Akdere, 2013).

In order to meet the goals of TD, formal and informal learning tools can be purposefully used in a blended environment. Formal training includes courses (online training, costly cases, illegal question) and in-house experts (webinars, meeting, interviews, virtual worlds); and informal learning tools include performance systems (glossary, YouTube/podcasting, class archive, real simple syndication, online bookmarking, job aids/manual), information repositories (company policy, HR procedure), and professional learning communities (online forums, wikis, social network sites, conference, quarterly meeting, blogs, Twitter). According Yoon and Lim (2010), such practices may influence workplace learning and performance.

In another study, Thomas and Akdere (2013) discussed how examining the role of collaborative media tools like Facebook and LinkedIn provides opportunities for HRD practitioners and scholars to identify and design best practices for the continuous improvement of organizations. They defined social media as some types of technologies that facilitate collaboration through several means and procedures, and organizations utilize them not only to increase their communication with customers, but also to improve learning and knowledge sharing within the organizations. They stated that the biggest fear of managers about the use of social media for learning is the lack of managers' understanding of social media's potential for knowledge sharing and the uncertainty that managers feel about the outcomes of using social media.

Although according to several researchers (e.g., Collings & Mellahi, 2009; Kim & McLean, 2014; Lewis & Hechman, 2006), the concept of talent development is derived from fully inclusive talent management typology in which every individual has the potential to be considered as talent. By identifying the tacit knowledge and abilities in people, organizations can unleash their potential and match them with the appropriate jobs. An additional feature of Twitter, according to Kwak, Lee, Park, and Moon (2010), is that Twitter has a feature that identifies the homophily among tweets. According to the Kwak et al., homophily is "a contact between similar people occurs at a higher rate than among dissimilar people" (2010, p. 594). Through the information gathered from this feature, organizations may find people who have proximity of ideas in order to put them in the same work group or distribute them within the organization in different groups based on an organization's strategies.

FUTURE TRENDS

We posit that HRD researchers and practitioners are interested in using trending technologies especially social media in developing talent, and it will give them insights for further research and new perspectives for practice. Researchers may explore the possibility of gaining a competitive advantage in organizations' talent management systems by applying

VHRD initiatives through utilizing social media as a strong and popular tool. For instance, Kwak et al. (2010) studied the power of Twitter in information sharing. An organizations can benefit from that power by creating Twitter accounts for both the organization and the employees who have not had Twitter accounts. They need to start from their employees and invite them to follow the organization on Twitter. Encouraging employees to be involved in this process may need to offer employees some benefits in exchange for their efforts: for example, devoting 30 minutes every day to attend a discussion and share an idea, or offer some kind of financial or recognition awards for the employees who have the most tweets or followers.

Mount and Martinez (2014) believed that employees could be motivated to attend and be involved in discussions and sharing, by offering them blended incentives. Intrinsic rewards such as fun, pride, satisfaction; extrinsic incentives such as monetary rewards; and status incentives such as community reputation and recognition could be some of the ways to motivate employees to get involve in social media activities. According to Mount and Martinez (2014), social media can help organizations gain a competitive advantage through data mining, identification of trends, idea storm, and building collective intelligence if motivated employees leverage social media into their work activities. In addition, the shortage in the workforce as a result of declining and retiring baby boomers, the preference of a new generation for social network sites, the flexible access to information, and the tendency to self-directed learning environment, forces organizations to change their talent management (TM) systems. It provide opportunities for researchers and practitioners in HRD to study and examine the positive and negative aspects of social media as a TM intervention in attracting and deploying potential talent, to develop a system in which organizations achieve optimum outcomes from utilizing such a huge, widespread, and low-cost tool.

There is no theoretical framework or models in HRD publications that show the relationship between using different social media and organizational/personal outcomes. Therefore, there is a need to conduct extensive research on the relationship between establishing organization or even worldwide social media tool like Twitter, LinkedIn, and Facebook for talent management purposes and individual/organization level outcomes such as performance, return on investment (ROI), training, knowledge sharing, brand awareness, satisfaction, commitment, tendency to leave or work, and many other outcomes. The risks, ethical and legal aspects of using social media as a main source of screening and recruiting employees would be considered as a future research idea.

The positive or negative impact of using social media could be examined through collecting data from the organizations that had accepted and used social media as their main talent management tool. Examining the effect of organization culture and management support for using social media as a key tool of TM could be examined. How the culture of an organization is important to supporting changes in traditional TM practices is a significant concern in social media and TM studies.

Exploring current and prospective employees' opinions toward using social media in different steps of talent management (e.g. screening, recruiting, developing, and retaining) is essential for understanding the job market point of view toward social media. By understanding what employees think of social media and how much they perceive social media as a helpful tool in their work, organizations can identify the needs and gaps in their social media strategies in order to motivate employees and utilize social media accordingly.

Last but not least, the effect of using social media for the purpose of increasing positive workplace outcomes may affect employees' life drastically (Yoon & Lim, 2010). For example, studying the effects (positive and negative) of using SM for the work-life balance of employees could be considered for future research that examines whether or not SM would influence workforce work-life balance in a positive way.

REFERENCES

Aral, S., Dellarocas, C., & Godes, D. (2013). Introduction to the special issue-social media and business transformation: A framework for research. *Information Systems Research, 24*(1), 3–13. Retrieved from http://dx.doi.org/10.1287/isre.1120.0470

Bennett, E. E. (2009). Virtual HRD: The intersection of knowledge management, culture, and intranets. *Advances in Developing Human Resources, 11*, 362–374.

Bennett, E. E. (2014). Introducing new perspectives on virtual human resource development. *Advances in Developing Human Resources, 16*(3) 263–280. doi:10.1177/1523422314532091

Boyd, D., & Ellison, N. (2008). Social network sites: Definition, history, and scholarship. *Journal of Computer Mediated Communication, 13*(1), 210–230.

Cappelli, P. (2009). Talent on demand: Managing talent in an age of uncertainty. *Strategic Direction, 25*(3).

Collings, D. G., & Mellahi, K. (2009). Strategic talent management: A review and research agenda. *Human Resource Management Review, 19*(4), 304–313. doi:10.1016/j.hrmr.2009.04.001.

Garg, R., & Telang, R. (2012). *To be or not to be linked on LinkedIn: Online social networks and job search*. Retrieved from http://ssrn.com/abstract=1813532

Kaplan, A. M., & Haenlein, M. (2009). Consumer use and business potential of virtual worlds: the case of second life. *The International Journal on Media Management, 11*(3/4), 93–101.

Kietzmann, J. H., Hermkens, K., McCarthy, I. P., & Silvestre, B. S. (2011). Social media? Get serious! Understanding the functional building blocks of social media. *Business Horizons, 54*(3), 241–251.

Kim, S., & McLean, G. N. (2012). Global talent management: Necessity, challenges, and the roles of HRD. *Advances in Developing Human Resources, 14*(566). doi:10.1177/1523422312455610.

Kwak, H., Lee, C., Park, H., & Moon, S. (2010). What is Twitter, a social network or a news media? *Proceedings of the 19th international conference on world wide web* (pp. 591–600). Raleigh, NC.

Lawler E. E. (2008), Strategic talent management: Lessons from corporate world. *Madison, WI: Consortium for Policy Research in Education*. Retrieved from http://www.smhc-cpre.org/wp-content/uploads/2008/06/strategic-talent-management-lawler-paper-may-08.pdf

Lewis, R., & Heckman, R. (2006). Talent management: A critical review. *Human Resource Management Review, 16*, 139–154.

Lin, Y. R., & Lazer, D. (2013). Watching how ideas spread over social media. *The MIT Press: Leonardo, 46*(3), 277–278. Retrieved from http://muse.jhu.edu/journals/len/summary/v046/46.3.lin.html

McWhorter, R. R. (2010). Exploring the emergence of virtual human resource development. *Advances in Human Resources. 12*(6), 623–631. doi:10.1177/1523422310395367

Mount, M., & Martinez, M. G. (2014). Social media: A tool for open innovation. *California Management, 56*(4),124–143.

Noe, A. R. (2010). *Employee training and development* (5th ed.). New York, NY: McGraw-Hill.

Nolan, H. (2009, May 26). New York Times 'social media editor' playing out exactly as suspected. Retrieved from http://gawker.com/5270593/newyork-times-social-media-editor-playing-out-exactly-as-suspected

Roberts. G., & Sambrook, S. (2014). Social networking and HRD. *Human Resource Development International.* doi:10.1080/13678868.2014.969504

Short, D. (2010). Foreword: Reflection on virtual HRD from a scholar-practitioner. *Advances in Developing Human Resources. 12*(6), 619–622. doi:10.1177/1523422310394788.

Solomon, M. (2010). E-learning: How to do it effectively. *Human Resources, 14*(6), 16–17.

Statista. (2015). Statistics and facts about Facebook and LinkedIn. Retrieved from https://www.statista.com/topics/951/linkedin/

Thomas, K. J., & Akdere, M. (2013). Social media as collaborative media in workplace learning. *Human Resource Development Review, 12*(3), 329–344. doi:10.1177/1534484312472331

Wang, J. (2012). Human resource development and technology integrationIn V. Wang (Ed.), *Encyclopedia of E-Leadership, Counseling and Training* (Vol. 2, pp. 391–407). Boca Raton, FL: Florida Atlantic University.

Yoon, S. W., & Lim, D. H. (2010). Systemizing virtual learning and technologies by managing organizational competency and talents. *Advances in Developing Human Resources, 12*(6), 715–727. doi:10.1177/1523422310394795

CHAPTER 10

TALENT DEVELOPMENT VIA COGNITIVE MEDIATION

Heidi Flavian

Education, as a general concept, comprises a process that begins with birth in order to allow people to develop and become independent individuals in a society. Different cultures educate differently, and yet there is a common, global final goal. The formal process of education is conducted in kindergartens and schools by professional educators. They make their best efforts to teach all students the required knowledge, and expect them to learn and achieve the goals set by the education policymakers in their respective countries. In middle and high school, students' achievements are also compared among different countries around the world via international exams. While assessing and comparing these achievement results, educators commonly ask questions as to their essence such as: Are students with high test-scores more talented than others? What are the roles of the educators throughout the learning process if everything is led by the students' talents? Can talent be changed? And lately, educators have dared to question the use of test scores by focusing on the idea that all students are born with talent, but society does not know how to expose and develop it through regular learning processes in school.

The idea that all people are born with talent but develop differently, think differently, and achieve different learning results has been raised

Talent Development and the Global Economy:
Perspectives from Special Interest Groups, pp. 155–170
Copyright © 2017 by Information Age Publishing
All rights of reproduction in any form reserved.

by a variety of psychology and education researchers for many years. Throughout the last century, Vygotsky (1927, in Kozulin, 1999), Feuerstein, Feuerstein, Falik, and Rand (2006), and Gardner (2011) developed different social-educational theories, all based on the understanding that social mediation plays a significant role in talent development. In contrast, Huyck and Passmore (2013) studied how the human brain develops and functions and did not agree with this sociocultural approach but claimed that talent development is linked entirely to biological factors. But for decades, researchers believed that the two fields of the science of brain function and development and the science of education and psychology were irrelevant to each other.

Nowadays researchers understand that although talent, cognition, and thinking originate from genetic sources, the most significant development occurs as a result of the variety of interactions with the environment in both formal and informal education settings (Grigaityte & Iacoboni, 2014). Currently, when social-educational theories such as those developed by Vygotsky, Feuerstein, and Gardner have a solid research basis, the education field welcomes opportunities to integrate them throughout the formal education process students undergo. Cooperation between researchers from different fields has promoted the development of cognitive theories, focusing more on how society can influence talent development rather than on the question of whether it is possible.

Feuerstein, Feuerstein, Falik, and Rand (2002) introduced during the 1960s what he considered to be an essential concept: structured mediation that would lead to a process of cognitive changes. The main idea was that through suitable human mediation processes, one's cognitive abilities and talent development could be improved significantly. For many years the approach of structured mediation was not acceptable, and educators used the concept of mediation with great caution. At present, educators use the term mediation to describe human interventions to improve cognitive and talent development (Mandikonza & Lotz-Sisitka, 2016). In this chapter, I will present three main approaches to mediation and talent development with examples of the various ways they can be better used among students. All three scholars, Vygotzky, Feuerstein and Gardner, believed that it is up to society to mediate and promote talent development. None of them referred to students' intelligence as a factor that either obstructs or enables talent development. They also did not accept the idea that students' talent successes could be predicted. Their main claim was that people should mediate the best they can to develop students' talents and thinking processes. Therefore, the reference through this chapter is to all students across a wide spectrum of intelligence—from students with cognitive special needs to gifted students. The presentation is chronological: first Vygotzky, who conducted his work at the beginning of the 20th century;

then Feuerstein, who began developing his theory in the mid-20th century; and finally Gardner, who developed his approach in the 1970s.

A WORD ON STUDENTS' COGNITIVE DIVERSITY

The diversity of students in schools causes educators to develop curricula in different subjects that allow all students to study. Education leaders usually develop curricula, defining main topics and expected achievements. Not only do they define the expected outcomes without knowing the students and the teachers, in some countries teachers are even evaluated by the success of their students. In addition, the mandatory teaching-learning curricula do not always change in a timely manner to keep abreast with changes in knowledge around the world (Schleicher, 2011). As a result, students undergo a variety of assessments that supposedly predict whether or not they have talent. Moreover, these assessment outcomes often lead to placement in study groups with labels such as gifted students, average students, or below average students. Fundamentally, educators develop curricula for all, making sure all students acquire the same basic knowledge. Thus, the focus is on teaching information rather than on developing everyone's talent.

The discussions in regard to talent development among students are usually kept for educators who teach and follow the groups of gifted students, justifying it by claiming that gifted students may get bored in school and teachers should challenge them more. But, should not all students be challenged? Moreover, the fear of frustration among students with cognitive special needs prevents most education leaders from demanding talent development and cognitive challenging of these students. The lack of cognitively challenging activities that develop everyone's talent basically evolves from a misunderstanding of fundamental concepts, such as thinking, learning, talent, cognitive difficulties, and special needs. Educators tend to group together thinking, learning, and talent development (Olszewski-Kubilus & Thomas, 2015), while referring to cognitive difficulties, special needs, and lack of talent as another group. Realistically, for some people with cognitive difficulties, the ways to develop their talent are very complicated. But, for the majority of the people with cognitive difficulties and special needs, suitable modification of the learning processes will enable development of their talent as well.

Most students with special needs are included in regular educational programs from kindergarten through school years, and even in higher academic studies in colleges and universities (Flavian, 2011). Therefore, the question nowadays is not whether or not to promote integration, but how to best promote learning among the more severely challenged students. The fact that some students may have cognitive difficulties should not lead one to assume that they have no talent. On the contrary, their cognitive challenges should lead educators to search for varied ways to keep developing their as yet unfulfilled talent (Levine, 2002). In many cases, educators do not try to challenge children who present learning difficulties because they do not believe these students have talent, and because they do not realize that the reasons the students have difficulties arise from their lack of cognitive tools and learning experiences (Feuerstein, Klein, & Tannenbaum, 1994; Levine, 2003). There are two basic conditions for providing a learning environment that promotes the talent development of all students: believing and understanding that (a) all students have talent, and (b) that educators can provide the proper learning paths for effective development by acquiring a variety of learning theories and approaches.

On the customary spectrum of learners, educators tend to locate gifted learners at the opposite end from the students with special needs. The source of this differentiation is linked to the traditional approach in which educators refer to gifted students as those born with more talent than others and who therefore do not have any cognitive difficulties. Recently, educators and researchers began using talent development in reference to a specific area of giftedness among learners (Olszewski-Kubilus & Thomas, 2015). This approach allowed the integration of educational domains, on the understanding that a person may be talented in one domain, but at the same time have some learning difficulties in others. Moreover, educators may understand learning processes from a broader perspective. Now, when they detect learning difficulties among their students, they have theoretical support to look for the strengths—the talents of the children—and develop their talents and thinking processes in ways that support the difficulties as well.

In recent years, there has been support for referring to giftedness from a narrow perspective, while referring to talent development as a process that integrates the variety of abilities one has, and that it is up to society to provide children with the opportunities to better develop their talents. For example, after investigating brain development and mathematical thinking, Dehaene, Spelke, Pinel, Stanescu, and Tsivkin (1999) claimed that the fields of language development and mathematical thinking should no longer be separated but integrated. At the same time, Butterworth (1999) described a case study in which a person was born with the mental inability to perform any mathematical thinking, but graduated university studies in psychology successfully. These and others encouraged other theoreticians, psychologists, and educators to base teaching and learning on the view of developing talent among all students.

VYGOTSKY'S PSYCHOLOGICAL THEORY OF COGNITIVE DEVELOPMENT

Lev Vygotsky (1896–1934) developed one of the most innovative psychological and learning theories of the 20th century (Kozulin, 2015). His interest in art and the humanities led him toward the understanding of psychology as a culture, and emphasized his belief in society's influences on talent development. Vygotsky claimed that most of the cognitive processes humans use are unique to humanity and can be developed only through human mediation. Since one acquires basic cognitive skills by learning from a variety of experiences, significant talent development can occur only through human mediators who mediate according to the culture they live in. This conclusion was developed from observing and comparing different learning interactions between animals and humans. The interactions between animals led to a process in which the younger generations learned from the adults what they should do and how to act in certain situations, and they were expected to repeat what they had learned in order to survive. Since among humans the younger generation must grow up to be leaders, they are expected to develop new skills to deal with new situations in life. According to Vygotsky, these new cognitive skills are proof of effective prior talent development.

Another component that emphasizes the role of human mediators in the process of high cognitive and talent development is the use of language. Language contributes to talent development through two main paths. The first perspective distinguishes humans from animals, in that language promotes communication while communication promotes mediation and learning. The second path is derives from communications: the more humans communicate, the richer and more complex their language becomes, and this forces them to use higher cognitive skills. Vygotsky's conclusion evolved from comparing cultural changes and language differences between different generations (Kozulin, 2015). Although we cannot compare the intelligence of the people who lived 100 years ago to those who live today, we can compare the differences in vocabulary, cultural tools, and the variety of communication tools.

One of the main concepts used repeatedly in Vygotsky's theory is *mediation*. The distinction between coincidental mediation and what Vygotsky meant for development of cognitive functions and talent is characterized by the combination of three components that build talent development: use of physical tools, use of symbolic tools, and human mediation. Vygotsky hypothesized that the use of new and different physical tools may have a reciprocal effect on the development of human talent due to the fact that new experiences require new cognitive tools. The symbolic tools are culture-related, and can be used effectively only via proper mediation.

Human mediation leads to acquisition and internalization of the symbolic tools that allow humans to regulate and shape their own cognitive and behavioral processes (Kozulin, 2015). Human mediation, according to Vygotsky, is focused on one's talent development and the improved use of high level cognitive functions both while communicating with others and while conducting internal thinking processes.

From their study on cognitive development, Shayer and Adhmi (2010) concluded that basing mathematics lessons on Vygotsky's social mediation significantly improved the use of cognitive functions among young children. They based mediation on the use of high level, yet clear language, and group studies alongside individual learning focusing on cognitive processes.

THE ROLE OF EDUCATORS ACCORDING TO VYGOTSKY'S PSYCHOLOGICAL THEORY

Talent development, according to Vygotsky's psychological theory, can be conducted by any human mediator and with all children. Therefore, educators who set themselves a goal of promoting talent development throughout curricula must integrate the core of this theory into their teaching practices. The understanding that culture serves as a key stimulus to learning is the basis for the continuum of talent development. Educators must have knowledge of their students' culture in order to relate learning processes to reality, along with providing them with proper cognitive tools that allow them to further study their culture on their own. Language, which is inseparable from culture and therefore from learning, should be used properly and accurately by mediators, keeping in mind that high cognitive functions are developed through the use of accurate forms of language.

The notion of mediation should guide educators by focusing on developing specific cognitive functions to improve talent development in general. Mediators have to plan learning experiences that will provide opportunities for collaborative learning in groups along with individual learning, all based on proper language, cultural relevance, and the need to activate high cognitive functions.

Feuerstein's Mediated Learning Experience (MLE) Theory

Reuven Feuerstein (1921–2014) developed the cognitive modifiability approach alongside his mediated learning experience (MLE) theory while working with children as a clinical, developmental and cognitive psychologist. During the 1950s and 1960s, he worked with children who had emigrated from Europe to Israel and discovered that when standard intelligence tests were administered to these children they did poorly, but if guided through the question-answer format by a mediator, the children's performance improved dramatically. From this experience he questioned beliefs regarding the stability of intelligence, and posited that cultural differences affect learning processes. He developed new methods of evaluation and new teaching tools that searched for cognitive flexibility and talent development among all children. This period was also seminal to the development of the hypothesis concerning low-functioning children and their potential for change. Through research, he discovered that the key to meaningful instruction for all children is the mediated relationship.

Basing his work on the belief that mediation is the tool for everyone's talent development, he developed the dynamic assessment of cognitive modifiability, the instrumental enrichment program focused on improving cognitive functions, and defined 12 mediation criteria to promote proper cognitive modifiability (Feuerstein, Feuerstein, Falik, & Rand, 2002).

Understanding from his work and studies that with proper mediation all children's cognitive functions can be improved, Feuerstein referred to intelligence as a dynamic and changeable factor, while focusing on human mediation as the core process driving the changes (Feuerstein et al., 2006). He motivated all caregivers and educators to believe in everyone's cognitive modifiability and developed five hierarchic stages to achieve this belief. The stages are: (1) that all children can improve their cognitive function and develop their talent, (2) that even children with deficient cognitive functions can improve and develop their talent, (3) as a result of the children's cognitive changes, mediators can change and develop their own cognitive functions and talent, that mediators can cause children to believe in themselves and in their ability to develop their talent, (4) and finally, (5) the belief that mediators can cause society to believe in children's cognitive modifiability.

In order to allow mediators to plan mediated interactions and to follow mediatees' talent development, Feuerstein categorized the thinking process into 28 specific cognitive functions through the input, elaboration, and output stages. The cognitive functions are the mental conditions essential to the existence of thinking operations and any type of behavioral functions, and they are all modifiable through proper mediation (Feuerstein et al., 1994). All 28 cognitive functions are defined from two perspectives: a positive definition that presents proper function and a negative perspective that refers to an inefficient thinking process caused by a deficient cognitive function. In situations when children do not present learning results as expected, the mediator should look for the deficient cognitive functions that need to be mediated.

Construction of proper mediated interactions according to the MLE should adhere to the 12 mediation criteria Feuerstein defined. Through every mediated interaction, the mediator must plan when and how to integrate the necessary criteria of mediation. Although the mediation process is flexible, and it is up to the mediator to moderate it, it is also mandatory to integrate at least the first three criteria. The 12 criteria of mediation are: intentionality and reciprocity, transcendence, meaning, mediation for feelings of competence, self-regulation, sharing behavior, goal and challenge seeking, psychological individuation and differentiation, novelty and complexity, awareness of the potential for change, the search for positive alternatives, and the sense of belonging.

As described briefly, MLE theory is based on the belief that all people can improve their thinking processes and better develop their talent potential, if only they are mediated by those who believe in their ability to cognitively change.

THE ROLE OF EDUCATORS ACCORDING TO THE MLE

Although MLE theory developed through the multiplicity of his experiences with children who presented low cognitive function, Feuerstein intended MLE theory for comprehensive use, in the belief everyone's talent can be developed and improved. Feuerstein believed that through mediation, every child regardless of the initial level of cognition could always improve cognitive processes. That understanding and belief are the basis for educators.

While educators usually teach students in groups, Feuerstein, who based his theory on the influence of society, demanded that mediators look at each child individually. Individual mediation should occur both individually and in groups. Planning of mediated interactions is based on recognizing the efficiency of children cognitive functions. When a child presents an inefficient learning process, the mediator must focus on the specific deficient cognitive function and mediate toward improving that function. On the other hand, when working with gifted children, mediators should remember that cognition continuously develops throughout life. Therefore, even here mediators need to focus on the cognitive functions that can improve talent and thinking processes. In general, mediation planning should be targeted toward developing talent among all students by basing mediation on thinking processes, whereas the content that needs to be learned is only the stimuli for practicing thinking rather than the goal of learning.

GARDNER'S MULTIPLE INTELLIGENCES THEORY

Beginning his professional path as a psychologist, Gardner (2000) developed an interest in learning and educational processes, focusing on issues that are relevant to cultures all around the world. Understanding that all people can think and learn, but at the same time all proceed differently, led Gardner (2000) toward the development of his multiple intelligences theory. A review of recent research in neurobiology supports the core idea that there are specific areas in the brain that correspond to certain processes of cognition, and that some people use their brains differently while studying the same subjects and achieving the same results (Gardner, 2011). Other studies discovered a significant relationship between the development of academic skills, thinking processes, and talent in general while basing learning on the multiple intelligences theory (Fang-Mei, 2014). The main questions Gardner focused on concerned the uniqueness of each area in the brain, which he defined as a unique intelligence, and the variety of ways educators may use his approach to promote talent development among all students.

As a basis for his approach, Gardner insisted that the discussion of talent development from the educators' point of view should always begin by clarifying the goals of education. Defining the educational goals can make talent development a more efficient process. Moreover, Gardner claimed that efficient learning that develops from strengthening talent is based on avoiding educational goals that relate specifically to one culture or another, but still prepare individuals to be part of their society. From this point of view, basing learning development on adults' modeling for practicing learning, Gardner referred to two main educational goals that may guide all educators around the world as they develop students' talent and long-term thinking practices: assimilating the beliefs and values of the culture, and the learning process in general. From this viewpoint of social mediation, children can understand that the learning process has been developed to allow them to become part of society and is not just for school. Moreover, students will better cooperate and practice the thinking skills that promote their own talent development without looking for concrete and immediate results. Another core educational viewpoint that is integral to Gardner's theory is the acceptance of the educational process as a whole, in which various elements both utilize and influence the efficiency of one's talent development. The wholeness of the educational process on individuals' talent development is a result of the understanding that every member of society and every stimulus in a child's surroundings participates in the process.

The concept of *multiple intelligences* developed from questioning theories of cognitive psychology for many years (Gardner, 2011). Throughout the development of this theory, Gardner referred to all students in all cultures. The goal was to provide educators with the understanding of different learning processes from different points of view. Moreover, accepting the fact that each person is born with basic biological factors and talent that serve as the basis for learning, Gardner was influenced by Vygotsky's theory and adopted the approach that one's intelligence and talent can be significantly developed by ambient human mediation using content that is relevant to the learner. While some researchers claim that the varieties of intelligences are correlated one to another, Gardner claims that although there are some positive correlations, each intelligence has unique features that contribute to the overall talent development. Beyond knowing the definition of each intelligence, educators should understand and accept that, even when basing their learning on a specific intelligence, students may present their talents differently from one another.

The main seven intelligences presented and defined by Gardner (2011, pp. 77–292) allow educators to focus and follow talent development procedures among learners.

Verbal-Linguistic Intelligence

Verbal-linguistic intelligence presents one's ability to use proper language (words, signs, and symbols) throughout the process of thinking and communicating. Proper and efficient use of verbal-linguistic intelligence is expressed not only by the use of language, but by the complex understanding of the internal relations between all the components of the language. This intelligence allows students to understand language beyond the basic meaning of the words, by applying metalinguistic skills to reflect on their use of language. Verbal-linguistic intelligence is the most widely shared human competence across all areas in life from birth on. It is integrated in all levels of communication via reading and writing, and those whose verbal-linguistic intelligence is high functioning can clearly express themselves and their thoughts in writing and speech.

Musical Intelligence

Musical intelligence is the earliest one to emerge in humans. Beyond the particular added value of musical intelligence in one's life, it relates to and influences one's talent development in all areas (Gardner, 2011). However, not all humans make use of this basic talent and it is clear that the development of musical intelligence relies on the proper mediation received from one's surroundings. Most people agree on the principal constituent elements of music, whereas only experts distinguish between each aspect. The definition of musical intelligence refers to the capacity to discern pitch, rhythm, timbre, and tone. This intelligence also enables us to recognize, create, reproduce, and reflect on music, as demonstrated by composers, conductors, musicians, vocalists, and sensitive listeners (Fang-Mei, 2014). Although some educators believe that expert musicians have a unique intelligence that others may not share, there is often an affective connection between music and other intelligences. For example, verbal intelligence can be improves by understanding the different tones people use for express themselves. Nevertheless, interpersonal intelligence is based, among other components, on one's intelligence to understand the unique patterns and voice people use for communication.

Logical-Mathematical Intelligence

Understanding the logic behind procedures, organizing complex events and components logically with proper explanations, and using proper criteria while analyzing and conducting new challenges are just some of the capabilities people with a high level of logical-mathematical intelligence may present. Moreover, it includes the ability to calculate, quantify, consider propositions and hypotheses, and carry out complex mathematical operations. Developing this perspective of talent enables students to perceive relationships and connections, to use abstract, symbolic thought, and to use inductive and deductive thinking operations.

Spatial Intelligence

Gardner (2011) defined the core of spatial intelligence as the capacity to perceive the visual world accurately, to transform and modify initial perceptions, and to develop the ability to re-create aspects of one's visual experiences although the concrete stimuli may be absent. This intelligence is expressed also by including the ability to think in three dimensions, integrating mental imagery, spatial reasoning, image manipulation, and graphic and artistic skills. Students develop the spatial talent in a variety of life experiences, while learning academic skills such as reading and writing and while experiencing the events around them. Proper mediation for understanding the variety of relationships among events promotes the development of this intelligence.

Bodily-Kinaesthetic Intelligence

Till today, many discussions and studies have been conducted in order to better understand the prehistoric origins of bodily intelligence and its relation to cognitive functions. Unfortunately, despite scientific progress, the development of these skills and the mutual effects they have on one another are not universally accepted. According to Gardner (2000), bodily-kinaesthetic intelligence is presented when people manipulate objects and use a variety of physical skills to better understand events, to better express themselves, and to communicate with others. This intelligence also involves a sense of timing and the perfection of skills through mind-body unity. As for culture differences, the understanding and use of body language for communication and expression may be varied, but the essence of bodily-kinaesthetic intelligence is common to all.

Interpersonal Intelligence

The ability to understand social situations and to interact effectively with others is the core meaning of interpersonal intelligence. This perspective of people's talent also involves effective verbal and nonverbal communication, the ability to note distinctions among others, developing proper sensitivity to the moods and temperaments of others, and the ability to entertain multiple perspectives. Moreover, developing interpersonal intelligence requires behavioral flexibility in order to adjust to new situations.

Intrapersonal Intelligence

Whereas all the aforementioned intelligences present different ways to learn and express an understanding of surrounding events, the concept of intrapersonal intelligence refers to individuals' understanding and expression of the events for themselves. Intrapersonal intelligence focuses on people's capacity to understand their own thoughts and feelings and to use such knowledge in planning and directing their lives. This intelligence involves not only an appreciation of the self, but also of the human condition.

PROMOTING TALENT DEVELOPMENT ACCORDING TO THE THEORY OF MULTIPLE INTELLIGENCES

The process of talent development among all students according to the theory of multiple intelligences relies more than anything else on educators' understanding that children are born with all types of intelligences, and it is up to the mediators around them to see how far that talent will be developed. Thus, educators should be willing to plan their teaching processes with reference to all seven intelligences. Understanding the theory, the components, and the complexity of multiple intelligences may be a starting point for implementing it throughout curricula. But, in order to be able to develop students' talent accordingly, educators should also better know their students. As mentioned earlier, although all students can basically use all seven intelligences, they need proper mediation to do so. Educators need to challenge their students' cognitive development by planning learning activities appropriately.

According to the theory of multiple intelligences, proper lesson planning should be done while mediating the subjects using aspects of all seven intelligences. Only then can educators refer to three main groups: students with cognitive challenges, students who study and complete all their learning as expected, and gifted students who complete all their studies easily but do not present any particular talent development. For students with cognitive challenges, the starting point will be to identify their most efficient intelligence, and after developing a proper sense of competence, to introduce them, one by one, to all the other intelligences. This process will allow them to acquire other alternatives for learning, so when they face a challenge they will have an alternative cognitive tool to overcome it. On the other end of the spectrum, the gifted students need to be challenged as well. Usually, they adopt a certain method of learning, but they do not challenge themselves and therefore do not develop their other talents efficiently. Educators must present learning processes based on the intelligences these students avoid, and challenge them for flexibility and talent development in new learning situations. For the third and largest group of students, educators must prepare learning processes that demand the use of all seven intelligences. This is because students who are use to "doing okay" at school, but are not familiar with their ability to use different intelligences, will not develop their full talent efficiently.

CONCLUSION

The mystery of talent development has been studied from different perspectives over the last century by several researchers. While some researchers have been examining brain function and development, others have been studying the psychological point of view and the role of society in one's cognitive and talent development. As studies continue and the search to understanding the procedure of talent development strengthens, it becomes clear that the more this domain is studied and the more the results are implemented, the more questions have arisen. Another conclusion emphasizes that talent development depends on both biological and cultural effects. Therefore, researchers should cooperate while planning, conducting, and implementing studies.

The three approaches of Vygotsky, Feuerstein, and Gardner presented in this chapter should serve as a basis for all educators who wish to develop students' talents. All three researchers led educators along a common path of motivating people to develop children's talents through a variety of mediation processes. Educators should base their teaching-learning sessions on such mediation processes, keeping in mind that all children have talent and that it is up to the mediators to what extent that talent will be developed.

Although it seems to be easier and simpler to promote talent development among gifted children, it is not so. The essence of cognitive development—thinking processes, brain development, and the mediation that children experience from birth—are all different from one child to another. These differences cause the mediation for talent development to be unique for each one. Furthermore, when teaching children who understand immediately or have great grades in all subjects, educators do not try to follow their thinking processes in order to better mediate for talent development. In contrast, while teaching children with learning challenges, educators who believe in their learners' inner talent will search for new mediation processes that will allow the children to learn better and develop their talent more efficiently.

Some educators may claim that the fact that Vygotsky, Feuerstein, and Gardner developed their theories in regard to learning, cognitive, and talent development many years ago renders their theories irrelevant for our era. My approach, as presented in this chapter, is that the current era only strengthens their theories. In contrast to learning programs that rely on specific content, their theories rely on thinking processes. Contents may change their relevance according to an era, culture, age, and other factors, while talent has been developing since the beginning of humanity among all people who are motivated and mediated to think, and it continues to do so. Following this approach, educators in many countries base their teaching on national curricula that stress the development of cognitive skills students will need in their future lives.

Implementing educators and psychologists' beliefs that talent development can and should be universal, it is up to the mediators how efficiently this development will be carried out, and it should be structured throughout education processes from early childhood. The first step toward this process will be providing proper knowledge to all teachers, who must learn that talent does not develop by itself, but rather simultaneously alongside thinking-skills development and mainly when mediators have the intention to develop it. Therefore, during teacher-training programs, teachers also need to develop their expertise in how they can teach thinking skills across the curriculum (Sanz de Acedo Lizarraga, Sanz de Acedo Baquedano, & Oliver, 2010).

After learning and researching the domains of talent, thinking, and cognition development, a better understanding of the role of parents and teachers as mediators for promoting talent development can begin. Only then can proper, structured mediation programs be planned as they should, since nonstructured mediation has less effectiveness, if any, on talent development (Haywood, 2004). Although the idea of developing *structured mediation programs* may seem inadequate and isolated from the student's uniqueness, this is not the objective. Structured mediation programs are based on the understanding that all children can develop their talents with proper structured mediation, but the mediation process must proceed according to students' interests, culture, prior knowledge, thinking skills, and motivation to learn. Educators need to know their students before conducting the mediation process. Moreover, although the leading concept is to base mediation on a structured program, it should also be flexible and the mediators should change it according to the development of each student.

Herein, I have presented three main approaches: Vygotsky's psychological theory of cognitive development, which focused on the powerful influence society has on cognitive and talent development; Feuerstein's mediated learning experience theory, which emphasizes the ability of human mediators not just to develop one's talent, but also to overcome congenital cognitive difficulties; and Gardner's multiple intelligences theory based on the assumption that all people have talent, but their thinking processes are different and therefore educators can develop children's talent by approaching the mediation process from different viewpoints. To these three approaches, which have already been implemented successfully through a variety of curricula, educators should add their own knowledge, experiences, and mainly their belief in talent development. Then they should develop new opportunities to develop talent among all their students.

REFERENCES

Butterworth, B. (1999). Counting on our brain. *Nature, 401*(6749), 114–115. doi:10.1038/43558

Dehaene, S., Spelke, E., Pinel, P., Stanescu, R., & Tsivkin, S. (1999). Sources of mathematical thinking: Behavioral and brain-image evidence. *Science, 284*(5416), 970–974.

Fang-Mei, T. (2014). Exploring multiple intelligences. *The Journal of Human Resource and Adult Learning, 10*(1), 11–21.

Feuerstein, F., Klein, P., & Tannenbaum, A. (1994). *Mediated learning experience (MLE)*. Jerusalem, IL: International Center for Enhancement of Learning Potential (ICELP).

Feuerstein, R., Feuerstein, R. S., Falik, L., & Rand, Y. (2002). *The dynamic assessment of cognitive modifiability.* Jerusalem, IL: International Center for Enhancement of Learning Potential.

Feuerstein, R., Feuerstein, R. S., Falik, L., & Rand, Y. (2006). *The Feuerstein instrumental enrichment program. An Intervention program for cognitive modifiability.* Jerusalem, IL: International Center for Enhancement of Learning Potential.

Flavian, H. (2011). Teachers with learning disabilities: Modelling coping mechanisms in the classroom. *Education Canada, 51*(3), 31–33

Gardner, H. (2000). *The disciplined mind.* New York, NY: Penguin.

Gardner, H. (2011). *Frames of mind. The theory of multiple intelligences.* New York, NY: Basic Books.

Grigaityte, K., & Iacoboni, M. (2014). The brain prize 2014: Complex human functions. *Science & Society, Trends in Neurosciences, 1096,* 1–3.

Haywood, C. H. (2004). Thinking in, around and about the curriculum: The role of cognitive education. *International Journal of Disability, Development and Education, 51*(3), 231–252.

Huyck, C. R., & Passmore, P. J. (2013). A review of cell assemblies. *Biological Cybernetics, 107,* 263–288.

Kozulin, A. (1999). *Vygotsky's psychology.* Cambridge, MA: Harvard University Press.

Kozulin, A. (2015). Vygotsky's theory of cognitive development. In J. D. Wright (Ed.), *International encyclopedia of the social & behavioral sciences* (2nd ed., Vol 25, pp. 322–328). Oxford, England: Elsevier.

Levine, M. (2002). *A mind at a time.* New York, NY: Simon & Schuster.

Levine, M. (2003). *The myth of laziness.* New York, NY: Simon & Schuster.

Mandikonza, C., & Lotz-Sisitka, H. (2016). Emergence of environment and sustainability education (ESE) in teacher education contexts in southern Africa: A common good concern. *Educational Research for Social Change, 5,* 107–130.

Olszewski-Kubilus, P., & Thomas, D. (2015). Talent development as a framework for gifted education. *Gifted Child Today, 38*(1), 49–59.

Sanz de Acedo Lizarraga, M. L., Sanz de Acedo Baquedano, M. T., & Oliver, M. S. (2010). Psychological intervention in thinking skills with primary education students. *School Psychology International, 31,* 131–145.

Schleicher, A. (2011). *Building a high-quality teaching profession: Lessons from around the world.* OECD Publishing. Retrieved from http://dx.doi.org/10.1787/9789264113046-en

Shayer, M., & Adhmi, M. (2010). Realizing the cognitive potential of children 5–7 with a mathematics focus: Post-test and long term effects of a 2-year intervention. *British Journal of Educational Psychology, 80,* 363–379.

ABOUT THE AUTHORS

Michael Beyerlein is a professor in the Human Resource Development Graduate Program at Texas A&M University. Formerly, he was a professor and department head of organizational leadership and supervision at Purdue, and prior to that the founding director of the Center for Collaborative Organizations and professor of industrial/organizational psychology at the University of North Texas. His books, book chapters, and articles usually address the topics of teams and collaboration, creativity and innovation, knowledge management, and intangible capital. His research interests include team creativity and innovation science. His most recent edited book is *The Handbook for High Performance Virtual Teams* (2008) written with Jill Nemiro and others. He served as senior editor of the annual book series *Advances in Interdisciplinary Studies of Work Teams*, the book series *Collaborative Work Systems*, and the journal *Team Performance Management*. His project funding has come from the NSF, several additional government agencies, and companies such as Boeing, Shell, NCH, AMD, Intel, Raytheon, First American Financial, Westinghouse, and Xerox.

Misha Chakraborty is working toward a PhD in human resource development at Texas A&M University. She holds a master's degree in human resource development from the University of Houston. She was awarded the Gold Medal and Dean's Prize for Academic Excellence during her undergraduate study. She received her undergraduate degree and postgraduate diploma from Queen Margaret University and Thames Valley University, United Kingdom. Her research interests include emotional intelligence, career development, distance learning, leadership, diversity, and organizational development. She is presently a graduate assistant at Texas A&M University. In this current role she supports the faculty at Texas A&M University in designing and delivering online classes. She is also involved in voluntary services to raise money for underprivileged children in developing countries.

Shannon Deer is a PhD candidate at Texas A&M University in educational human resource development with a specialization in adult education, and serves as the director of the full-time MBA program for Mays Business School at Texas A&M. Deer earned her master's degree in accounting from Texas A&M and is a licensed certified professional accountant. She has a background in business with experience auditing large Securities and Exchange Commission filers. She has translated her business experience into the classroom with more than 10 years of experience at Mays Business School developing and teaching a wide variety of accounting and finance courses, including some focused on the energy industry. Her research and teaching includes executive education that emphasizes sustainable business practices in the energy industry with regard to people, planet, and profit. Deer's research interests focus on the development of sustainable solutions for social problems. Her current line of research is investigating solutions to human trafficking. Deer is the recipient of numerous teaching awards, including the Association of Former Students Distinguished Teaching Award, the Ernst & Young Teaching Excellence Award, and the Baggett Teaching Award. She was honored to serve as a Fish Camp namesake in the summer of 2013 (a freshman orientation camp), one of the university's highest honors.

Khalil M. Dirani is an associate professor and program chair for the education and human resource development (HRD) program in the Department of Educational Administration and Human Resource Development at Texas A&M University. Dirani's research focus is on international HRD, learning organizations in Lebanon and the Middle East region, leadership and talent development, and the transfer of learning practices and theories across cultures. He developed the Arabic version of the Dimensions of the Learning Organization Questionnaire (Watkins & Marsick 1993), which was implemented by Arab scholars in Lebanon, Jordan, Saudi Arabia, and Egypt. Dirani's articles have appeared in both research and professional publications such as *Human Resource Development Quarterly, Human Resource Development International, International Human Resource Management, Advances in International Management,* and *European Journal for Training & Development.* Most recently, he co-edited a book on leadership development in emerging market economies. Dirani, teaches courses related to his research interests including, career development, training and development, evaluation, research methods, and statistics. In May 2017, he took a group of students to Dubai, UAE, to study HED practices in different organizational settings. Dirani serves his community and the field of HRD in different leadership capacities. In addition to being the chair of his program area, he serves on different committees at the department, college, and university level. Dirani served as a board member for the Academy of Human Resources Development (AHRD) from 2013 to 2016 and has served on the AHRD ethics committee since 2014. He also serves on three different journal boards and as a reviewer of manuscripts for seven journals.

Tomika W. Greer, PhD, is an associate instructional professor of human resource development in the College of Technology at the University of Houston. Greer has also served as program manager for the undergraduate HRD program and currently coordinates the undergraduate HRD internship program at the University of Houston. She is also a member of the editorial board for *Human Resource Development Review*. Greer's research focuses on trends and challenges associated with career development for women; implementation and outcomes of "family-friendly" organizational policies and programs; and curriculum, pedagogy, and the outcomes of academic programs in human resource development.

Soo Jeoung "Crystal" Han is currently a PhD candidate in the Department of Educational Administration and Human Resources at Texas A&M University. She received her master's in human resource development at Texas A&M and earned her bachelor's in English education from Korea University. She worked in business and academic institutions in South Korea for more than five years. Her research interests reflect her diverse work experience including the field of virtual team collaboration, cross-cultural team diversity, shared leadership development of teams, and global/women leadership. She has published several SSCI journals and book chapters in the field of collaborative learning, team leadership, and e-learning.

Yun-Hsiang Hsu, assistant professor, is from the Institute of Law and Government at the National Central University, Taiwan. He received his master's degree in demography from the University of California, Berkeley, in 2006, and his PhD in public policy and management from The Ohio State University in 2013. His specialization is policy analysis with a focus on workforce development. His publication topics include collaborative arrangements, apprenticeship, youth employment, employment service, and performance indicators. He has received several grants, including a Fulbright Scholarship and teaching grant, and has been commissioned by a wide range of government agencies, such as the National Development Council, Workforce Development Agency, Department of Labor, and Council of Aboriginal Peoples in Taiwan. Currently, he is funded by the Ministry of Science and Technology (Taiwan) for a 3-year project on public employment service for disconnected youth. This project intends to understand the impact of performance indicators on first-line officers for their selection of clients, who are the disconnected youth. An experimental design is applied to the officers in public employment agencies, grouped by short-term and long-term performance measures. Their attitude in delivering service and the labor market outcomes among disconnected youth are tracked in a 3-year period.

Beverly J. Irby serves as associate dean for academic affairs, College of Education and Human Development at Texas A&M University. She earned her EdD from the University of Mississippi in 1983. She joined the Department of Educational Administration and Human Resource Development at Texas A&M University as a full professor in September 2013, has been on the approved graduate faculty there since 2001, and has developed and taught courses in research and curriculum for special programs, educational administration, instructional leadership, and research. She has earned the reputation as an excellent professor, has mentored students, and has garnered numerous research awards. She was selected as a national UCEA David Clark Scholar Mentor and a two-time Piper Professor Nominee. She received a graduate student scholarship and the Brown and Irby Center for Research and Doctoral Studies in Educational Leadership is named in her honor at Sam Houston State University, Huntsville, Texas. Irby's research focus includes social responsibility for instructional leadership; theory development/validation; women's leadership; gender equity; early childhood, bilingual/ESL, gifted, and science education; online learning; reflective practice portfolios; international leadership; principal and teacher evaluation/professional development; program evaluation; and various research techniques including bricolage. A national and international speaker, she and her research group have developed studies and garnered more than $35 million in grant funding. She developed the Hispanic Bilingual Gifted Screening Instrument and the synergistic leadership theory. Irby, who has been a Texas State University System Regents Professor since 2009, also has received several awards and honors.

Shinhee Jeong is a doctoral candidate in the Department of Educational Administration and Human Resource at Texas A&M University. She previously worked as a program manager and researcher at Korea Labor Education Institute and Korea Research Institute of Vocational Education and Training. Her research interests include global leadership, team leadership, work engagement, and organizational knowledge creation in OD, and informal learning in the area of Training and Development. She has conducted various quantitative/qualitative studies and published her works in several SSCI journals and book chapters.

Sehoon Kim, PhD, is an assistant professor of human resources in the School of Business at the University of Wisconsin, Platteville. He earned his doctorate in human resource development from Texas A&M University, and has previously worked in the private sector as an HRD practitioner. His published and current research topics, based on a human development perspective, fall into three major streams: employee well-being, talent development, and international HRD. He has published in major academic journals, including *Adult Education Quarterly, Human Resource Development Review,* and *International Journal of Human Resource Management.* He previously received the Best Paper Award from the *European Journal of Training and Development* and the Cutting Edge Award from the Academy of Human Resource Development Conference.

Hae Na Kim obtained her PhD and master's degrees from the Workforce Development and Education Program specializing in human resources development (HRD) and adult learning at the Ohio State University (OSU) in Columbus. During her academic journey at OSU, she served as an instructor, a graduate teaching associate, and a graduate research associate. She has presented her research at Academy of Human Resource Development (AHRD) conferences and the University Forum for Human Resource Development. She has made contributions to AHRD conferences as a reviewer and session host. Originally from South Korea, she earned her bachelor's degree from Sookmyung Women's University in Seoul, and her master's of public affairs degree from Indiana University's School of Public and Environmental Affairs (SPEA) in Bloomington, Indiana. Also, she studied as an exchange student at York University in Toronto, Canada. Before joining OSU, she worked for the Human Resources Development Service of Korea (HRD Korea) under the Ministry of Employment and Labor of Korea. When she worked for HRD Korea, governmental officials at the Ministry of Employment and Labor recommended that she should continue her studies and major in HRD for her PhD degree. She received the John Coné Membership Scholarship from the Association for Training and Development and worked for the International Labor Organization as a consultant. Also, she interned at the Human Center of Samsung Life Insurance in South Korea and at the Citizens Network for Foreign Affairs in Washington, DC. Her recent research interests include organizational culture, career development, gender issues in HRD, mentoring and coaching, global HRD, and German dual training.

Fredrick Muyia Nafukho serves as a professor and associate dean for faculty affairs, College of Education and Human Development at Texas A&M University. Nafukho earned his PhD in human resource development from Louisiana State University, his master's in economics of education and his bachelor's degree in business studies and economics from Kenyatta University, Kenya. He attended Harvard's Management Development Program offered by Harvard Institutes for Higher Education. Nafukho has received numerous awards in recognition of his scholarship including the Fulbright Scholarship in 1996; Distinguished International Scholar Award, Louisiana State University in 1997; Arkansas Business Teacher Educator of the Year Award in 2004; Cutting Edge Award for the Outstanding Papers, Academy of Human Resource Development (with his student Carroll C. Graham) in 2005; Outstanding New Faculty Award, CEHD at Texas A&M University in 2008; and the Carnegie African Diaspora Fellowship in 2017. Nafukho's research focuses on educational policy analysis within international and comparative education, investment in human capital development, emotional intelligence and leadership development, organizational development and change, evaluation in organizations, transfer of learning, organizational learning, and e-learning.

Katherine M. Najjar is an instructor in the Department of Educational Administration at the University of Nebraska, Lincoln. She has taught classes in qualitative research methods, higher education finance, and K-12 finance. She is an assistant editor of the *Journal of Women in Educational Leadership*. Najjar worked for more than 20 years in the business world, and currently volunteers as an ELL tutor with a nonprofit organization. Her research interests explore ways that low-skilled migrant and refugee women access the workforce; how human/social capital and growth mindsets are developed through community engagement; and the economic impact of high-skilled migration in small to mid-sized communities.

Fatemeh Rezaei is a doctoral student in the HRD program at Texas A&M University. She has a bachelor's degree in mining engineering and a master's degree in international marketing from the University of Tehran, Iran. She received her second master's degree in human resource development in 2014 from Texas A&M University. She worked as a business consultant and researcher before coming to the United States in 2014. She is currently working as a teaching assistant at the Department of Educational Administration and Human Development, Texas A&M University. She cares about people and always is fascinated by their unique and inspirational stories. As an HRD researcher and future practitioner, she is passionate about finding cost-effective and innovative methods of learning and knowledge sharing that would unleash individual inner talent and improve organizations' productivity and effectiveness. She believes every person possess unique qualities and talents, and that by including all people, extraordinary and powerful teams will be built full of outstanding, creative, and happy people who can make dreams come true.

Richard J. Torraco is an associate professor in the Department of Educational Administration at the University of Nebraska, Lincoln. He is a faculty member in the educational leadership and community college leadership programs, and conducts research and teaching in workforce and human resource development as well as community college leadership. He has served as a journal editor of *Human Resource Development Review* and as the vice president for research for the Academy of Human Resource Development. Torraco's research examines the postsecondary education needs of academically underprepared, low-income, and disadvantaged students, and the persistence of working poor families and economic inequality in the United States. He teaches graduate courses (both in the classroom and on the Internet) in organization development and change, workforce development, and in administrative, organization and management theory. He has managed workplace health and safety programs and has served as an education and workforce development consultant to industry, business, and nonprofit organizations for more than 25 years.

Minerva D. Tuliao is a PhD candidate in the Department of Educational Administration at the University of Nebraska, Lincoln. She holds a master's degree in industrial-organizational psychology. Prior to pursuing doctoral studies, she spent 7 years as a human resource and organization development practitioner in higher education institutions, and in the finance and information technology sectors. Her research interests include examining the human resource, career, and workforce development issues of adult immigrants and refugees.

Jill Zarestky is an assistant professor in the adult education and training program in the School of Education at Colorado State University. Zarestky earned a PhD in educational human resource development specializing in adult education from Texas A&M University, and a master's degree in computational and applied mathematics from the University of Texas, Austin. Zarestky has more than 15 years of experience teaching mathematics and education courses in a variety of higher education contexts ranging from classes for first-year students to advanced doctoral courses, small seminars to large lectures using various formats including traditional face-to-face, hybrid, and fully online. Prior to her appointments in education, she was part of the faculty in the Department of Mathematics at Texas A&M University and worked for a number of years in educational publishing.

Zarestky's research interests include nonformal and community-based education, particularly in the context of international nongovernmental and nonprofit organizations; science, technology, engineering, and mathematics (STEM) education; and issues of feminism, globalization, and social justice. Zarestky also serves as the secretary of the American Association of Adult and Continuing Education.

0 1341 1717354 9

CPSIA information can be obtained
at www.ICGtesting.com
Printed in the USA
LVOW13s2329131217
559455LV00007B/18/P

9 781681 239972